The
P R O V I N C E T O W N
Artists Cookbook

by Christopher Busa
and Gillian Drake

A B I N G D O N ◆ P R E S S

For my father, Peter Busa, who said,
''The question, 'How do you cook?' reminds
me of the question, 'How do you paint?' ''
— C.B.

In memory of a dear friend, Barbara Mayo
— G.D.

We wish to thank the artists of
Provincetown for their cooperation
in producing this book.

Special thanks to William Evaul, Director of
the Provincetown Art Association and
Museum, for making available archival files on
Provincetown artists, indispensable in writing
the artists' capsule biographies.

Copies of this book may be ordered from
ABINGDON PRESS
Box 35, Provincetown, MA 02657

$9.95 plus $1.50 handling

*Write to the above address for other titles
by the same publisher.*

The Provincetown Artists Cookbook
was compiled by
Christopher Busa and Gillian Drake

Text: Christopher Busa
Design and Production: Gillian Drake
Production Staff: Karl Davis,
   Michael Leavenworth

Printed by
Shank Painter Printing Company
Provincetown, MA

CONTENTS

In the brilliant clear Cape light, circa 1930, spellbound students watched hushed while Charles Hawthorne demonstrated the lessons he verbalized. He urged students to spend their lifetime in hard work with a humble mind, the artist developing himself as he develops the beauty he sees. This is the basic artist's recipe for his own esthetic diversity. Thousands of artists have been attracted to Provincetown since the turn of the century, and today its resident artist population makes it the nation's largest art colony.

Photo by George Yater, courtesy of the Provincetown Art Association and Museum.

This book is inspired by the idea that artists are mere mortals, and have to eat like all of us. Food, like sex and shelter, is essential to human life. Art is not. We decided to begin at the beginning, not with art, but with what artists ate.

The 50 artists in this book represent a cross-section of contemporary Provincetown artists. Some live elsewhere and return for summers on the Lower Cape. Some are year round residents who pride themselves on the length of time that has passed since they crossed the bridge at Cape Cod Canal, where the Cape is severed from the mainland. Some have the city in their blood, others the country. Like the artists themselves, their recipes are diverse. Almost all use inexpensive ingredients, often fresh seafood simply prepared and slightly exotic. The instructions are straight-forward, with clear emphasis on a key quality. A little nonsense is used sparingly like salt. Many of the recipes were stolen from some good time in the artist's life when he had to make do with less. Sometimes a parent is the source of a special recipe. Some recipes serve crowds. There is a ritual use of alcohol. Implicated in the organic cycle, artists eat and drink as they make art, individually, but with the desire to share. Too diverse individually to be gathered as a group, they appear here at an ideal banquet.

The Family Table in the candlelit brick cellar of Ciro and Sal's restaurant, circa 1955. Ciro and Sal's was started by artists for artists. They found unity in food. An early advertisement announced, "Neo-classicists, post-impressionists, proto-cubists, pseudo-symbolists, anti-abstractionists and even unreconstructed dadaists all agree: Ciro and Sal's Meatball Sandwiches are MASTERPIECES."

As an older artist, Elise Asher remains youthful. Her white hair is radiant like platinum, her eyes dance with inward light as if her mind's eye saw sunlight fractured upon moving waters (this is true even in New York City where she lives in the winter, far from her summer home in Provincetown), and her skin glows with good health maintained over a lifetime. She has lived her life freely as an artist, first as a poet who published in celebrated small magazines such as *Poetry* and *Partisan Review*, culminating in the 1955 volume *The Meandering Absolute*, then, after an interlude living on the California coast perched on the cliffs with "dismaying drops

into that wild sea," where a colony of seals lived, bred, and died in a closed society utterly unlike Provincetown, Asher began painting, incorporating references to calligraphy as a way of remembering her previous life as a poet. About the transition from poet to painter, she says, "I began to feel more and more the urge to immerse myself physically in the poems, in the handwritten process, until I found myself actually painting them, developing a calligraphic embodiment of the 'written poem.' "

In her earlier paintings, she drew upon a private mythology of birds, fishes, seals (her "creatures," she calls them), tending to deface these images with shiny squiggles of inflected nonsense, often gold or orange. A favored device was to draw upon a second surface, affixing a sheet of plexiglass to a completed image underneath. The surface is agitated, and layers of bright paint glitter like phosphorus on moonstruck water. Set usually in a fantasy landscape, her creatures dominate the painting, the scale childlike in the sense that the psychologically important subject is given greatest emphasis, often towering lonely on the horizon. But since returning to canvas, in the middle 60s, her paintings and drawings have shifted their creative impulse, depicting less a fantasy world than a world of metaphysical reality. Recently she spent two years developing a series of paintings based on an elegiac poem, "The Long Boat," by Stanley Kunitz, Asher's husband. The poem is about the ship of death that each of us makes for ourselves as we near the end of our life, when our "dear ones on shore" have "already lost their faces" "in the rolling fog." The real pain of death is losing what one loves, yet the possession of that pain is like a food carried on an eternal journey. "The urgent poignancy of 'The Long Boat' has wholly enveloped me for over two years now," Asher says. "It has for me the force of visionary experience I seek to transform into a painterly vocabulary. I feel even the original metaphor itself ought to be transcended in order for the painting to stand on its own and apart from its point of origin."

"As If He Didn't Care", oil on canvas

Cream of Sorrel Soup

Especially good chilled, but can be served hot as well. Good for the spirit, it gentles and soothes a rising anger: a cocktail for Angels and Artists. This also makes an excellent sauce for fish.

1½ lbs. sorrel, approximately
2 quarts, approximately,
   of stock or other liquid, or
   1½ cans chicken or beef
   broth and 1 quart water
2 teaspoons salt
1 or more tablespoons
   lemon juice
2 tablespoons white or
   brown sugar
pinch of chives, chopped
   scallions, curry powder, or
   whatever seasoning you
   prefer (I prefer curry)
2 or 3 egg yolks
2 cups milk or
   very light cream

Wash the sorrel leaves and remove the stems, including the stem running through the center of each leaf. Drop the washed leaves into a large pot with the two quarts of liquid. Bring to a boil and then simmer for about 30 minutes. Add the lemon juice, salt, sugar, and that pinch of "whatever." Cook it all for about 10 minutes longer. Remove the pot from the heat and puree the soup by forcing it through a sieve; or use a blender or food processor. Now beat the egg yolks gently in a separate bowl and blend them with the milk or cream. Gradually add this to the hot soup, stirring as you pour. Do not let the soup boil. Serve chilled, garnished with chopped chives. Always stir the soup before dishing it out.

Bowen is a sculptor who arrived in Provincetown as a fellow at the Fine Arts Work Center in 1977. Now he is a yearround resident, living with his wife and ¨daughter in Ambrose Webster's former studio on Miller Hill Road.

Spare and frugal with his speech, he speaks his few words in a foreign accent of precise inflections, sounding sharp in the air, like sparks from small stones sent flying while hiking in heavy boots. He gives the impression of having settled in Provincetown just because it is so difficult to live here, and therefore, as a person familiar with difficulty, he is quite at home. Walking the soft sand of the winter beaches, somehow he is not far from the barren hills of North Wales. For years his work was decidedly influenced by his native Wales, especially its history. He grew up on rough terrain gouged with numerous slate quarries. Nearby was a shoe factory, and nearer the water was an active boatyard. With his father, an architect, Bowen explored various architectural ruins and ancient burial grounds. These sites, used by previous people long gone, were haunted by the evidence of human presence, however decomposed and fragmentary. This quality found expression in his subsequent sculpture, which incorporated found objects, encrusted and wrapped, stained or daubed with tar, suggesting the human equivalent of weathering.

In Provincetown, beachcombing the back shore and the bay flats, Bowen amassed huge collections of broken clay pipes, shoe leather, portions of porcelain dolls, corroded and bent forks, and other artifacts altered by exposure to innumerable tides. His sculpture became powerfully affected by his new environment. In one early work he compressed the soles of old shoes into a large round ball, covering the surface with overlapping leathers like so many footprints on a globe. In the 10 years he has lived here, he feels that his sculpture has moved from the dense, claustrophobic and forbidding to sculptures which are at once expansive and embracing. He describes his recent work: "Fragments of fishboxes held together with complex joinery over skeletal frames, looking sun-bleached like stranded ship's hulls or sections of whale carcasses, exposing their inner parts to the light and air."

Bowen shows regularly at the Jack Shainman Gallery in New York and at the Cherry Stone Gallery in Wellfleet. Increasingly, his difficult work is winning critical acclaim and is appearing in prominent collections across the country and overseas.

Knowing that "it is too hard to get blood in this country," Bowen declined to offer his recipe for blood sausage. He points out that MacMillan Wharf, between June and September, is a good place to catch squid at night. He himself reserves the squid ink for use in the studio as a medium for making drawings.

"Hiraethum," wood and chalk

Welsh-Portuguese Soup

dried red kidney beans,
   about a handful
1 large linguica sausage,
   sliced
   into ¼" pieces
1 medium onion, chopped
2 medium carrots, sliced
2 medium potatoes, chopped
   into ½-inch cubes
1 bunch of fresh kale (or
   1 package frozen kale),
   washed and chopped
1 medium can
   crushed tomatoes
1 small can tomato sauce
salt and pepper

Soak the beans overnight. The next day, drain them and add enough fresh water to cover. Saute onions and linguica, and combine all the ingredients in a pot and bring to a boil. Simmer the soup for at least two hours, adding more water and extra tomato sauce if necessary. Season to taste with salt and pepper. This soup tastes best when eaten the day after you make it. Serve it with Portuguese bread.

Squid Stew

4 to 6 good-sized squid
   (summer or bone)
⅔ cup olive oil
2 medium onions, diced
1 small can tomato sauce
   (not puree)
1 garlic clove,
   peeled and pressed
2 medium carrots, diced
¾ cup chopped mushrooms

Clean the squid* and wash them thoroughly. Cut the meat into thin strips. If the tentacles are large, each group can be split.

Saute the onions in olive oil, then add all the other ingredients and bring them to a boil. Turn down the heat and simmer the stew for 3 to 4 hours.

Add water if a thinner consistency is desired.

*Refer to pages 36 or 105 for instructions on cleaning squid.

Gillian Drake

Before summering in Provincetown for the first time in 1976, when he began to take the photographs that would be published in *Cape Light,* perhaps the most-praised and best-selling book of color photographs ever published, Joel Meyerowitz had earned a reputation as a black-and-white street photographer working in the tradition of Robert Frank and Cartier-Bresson. Immersed in the swift flow of crowds funneling through the streets of New York, Meyerowitz glided with the camera passing across his face, catching glimpses of simultaneous, yet separate subjects. In one, a boy in swimming trunks jumps off a low arching bridge in Central Park, while pedestrians pass by oblivious to a commercial photographer arranging the tripod on his hooded camera as two attractive models wait for him to take their picture.

After working at 1000th of a second with a hand-held 35mm camera, Meyerowitz bought a vintage Deardorff field-view camera, weighing 25 pounds and requiring a fixed tripod and the ritual of descending under a dark cloth to look at an image that is upside down and backwards. Less an antique than an alter ego, the camera was made in 1938, the same year that Meyerowitz was born. On the summer beaches of the Lower Cape, carrying his strange camera so casually over his shoulder, he became a familiar sight, the dark cloth of the hood trailing behind him, sometimes smoothing over the miles of footprints he made in the sand. When photographing, he found himself referring to the horizon line for orientation, the way astronauts, he points out, establish a "local vertical." Often making exposures of several minutes, his images seem contemplative and composed yet resonant with refractions of rich color, whose energy, like wind, is revealed by its effects on things. A speck of small boat or tiny people standing under vast skies on acres of tidal flats em incidental details rather than ostensible subjects, becoming minimal s for the charge of colored light on the total environment. In an interview npanying his *Cape Light* photographs, Meyerowitz says he wishes to atonal photographs," where the subject is everything in the frame and lated within a context. "It's the *risk* of taking a picture of the *small big space,*" he says, "that is exactly like the street pictures." ower, who married Meyerowitz in 1962 when he was a young tor at Albert Einstein College of Medicine, began her career as ring that she was less interested in the function of pottery

MEYEROWITZ

than in clay as a material. She began sculpting in clay, then drawing in pastel, never having drawn. Going from medium to medium as a self-taught artist, Bower found a similarity of touch in the materials. She tends to build the surfaces of her drawings with increasingly patterned strokes, as if the form she were drawing materialized only through a physical translation of the experience of looking. Working in a small studio adjacent to her East End bayside house, Bower says she tries to see past the surface for evidence of forms that don't appear to be there at first. Moonlight on open water or heatwaves above vanilla flats become second shapes, showing the effect of time on the contemplation of the artist, intensifying observations that are only latent in the moment. As *The New York Times* said in a review of her one-person show at the Victoria Monroe Gallery, Bower "seizes upon ephemera such as clouds or a wave and makes them solid entities."

Joel Meyerowitz

Sharing an aesthetic regard for the ephemeral and the small detail perhaps explains why Bower and Meyerowitz "definitely love desserts," as Vivian admits. A little sugar can't be all bad, considering that these ectomorphs stay in excellent trim, no doubt because they are uncommonly active, often taking 30-mile bicycle trips together and working up a dancing frenzy at parties.

Vivian Bower, pastel

Joel's Pecan Pie

1 cup sugar
½ cup dark Karo syrup
2 whole eggs beaten
1 tablespoon vanilla
1 tablespoon melted butter
1 cup chopped pecans

Cook sugar and corn syrup together gently. Mix with beaten eggs, butter and vanilla. Add pecans. Pour into a pie shell and bake for ½ hour to ¾ hour at 350°.

Vivian's Strawberry Tart

1 cup flour
¼ cup sugar
⅔ cup grated almonds
½ cup butter
fresh strawberries
red currant jelly

Mix flour, sugar and grated almonds. Cut in butter. Press into a 9'' form. Cool in refrigerator for one hour. Bake in 450° oven for 15 to 20 minutes.

When cool, fill with fresh strawberries — make your own design — and glaze top with heated red currant jelly.

Vivian's Key Lime Pie With Sliced Kiwi

Crust:
1½ cups graham cracker
  crumbs
¼ cup finely chopped
  almonds
1 teaspoon cinnamon
6 tablespoons melted butter

'lling:
  ng yolks
  try 4 yolks and fold in
  'l-beaten whites)
  n sweetened,
  ed milk
    lime juice
  es, depending

  'v chopped

For Crust: Mix all ingredients together thoroughly and press into a 10'' pie plate. Bake for 8 to 10 minutes in a 375° oven. Remove from oven and let cool. Reduce oven temperature to 350°.

For Filling: Beat yolks. Pour in condensed milk, stirring constantly. Add lime juice and rind. Pour into crust and bake for 15 minutes at 350°. When the pie is cool, thinly slice 2 or 3 kiwi to decorate top of pie.

than in clay as a material. She began sculpting in clay, then drawing in pastel, never having drawn. Going from medium to medium as a self-taught artist, Bower found a similarity of touch in the materials. She tends to build the surfaces of her drawings with increasingly patterned strokes, as if the form she were drawing materialized only through a physical translation of the experience of looking. Working in a small studio adjacent to her East End bayside house, Bower says she tries to see past the surface for evidence of forms that don't appear to be there at first. Moonlight on open water or heatwaves above vanilla flats become second shapes, showing the effect of time on the contemplation of the artist, intensifying observations that are only latent in the moment. As *The New York Times* said in a review of her one-person show at the Victoria Monroe Gallery, Bower "seizes upon ephemera such as clouds or a wave and makes them solid entities."

Joel Meyerowitz

Sharing an aesthetic regard for the ephemeral and the small detail perhaps explains why Bower and Meyerowitz "definitely love desserts," as Vivian admits. A little sugar can't be all bad, considering that these ectomorphs stay in excellent trim, no doubt because they are uncommonly active, often taking 30-mile bicycle trips together and working up a dancing frenzy at parties.

Vivian Bower, pastel

Joel's Pecan Pie

1 cup sugar
½ cup dark Karo syrup
2 whole eggs beaten
1 tablespoon vanilla
1 tablespoon melted butter
1 cup chopped pecans

Cook sugar and corn syrup together gently. Mix with beaten eggs, butter and vanilla. Add pecans. Pour into a pie shell and bake for ½ hour to ¾ hour at 350°.

Vivian's Strawberry Tart

1 cup flour
¼ cup sugar
⅔ cup grated almonds
½ cup butter
fresh strawberries
red currant jelly

Mix flour, sugar and grated almonds. Cut in butter. Press into a 9'' form. Cool in refrigerator for one hour. Bake in 450° oven for 15 to 20 minutes.

When cool, fill with fresh strawberries — make your own design — and glaze top with heated red currant jelly.

Vivian's Key Lime Pie With Sliced Kiwi

Crust:
1½ cups graham cracker
  crumbs
¼ cup finely chopped
  almonds
1 teaspoon cinnamon
6 tablespoons melted butter

Filling:
6 egg yolks
  (or try 4 yolks and fold in
  2 well-beaten whites)
14 oz. can sweetened,
  condensed milk
½ cup fresh lime juice
  (about 4 limes, depending
  on size)
2 teaspoons finely chopped
  lime rind
2 or 3 kiwi fruits

For Crust: Mix all ingredients together thoroughly and press into a 10'' pie plate. Bake for 8 to 10 minutes in a 375° oven. Remove from oven and let cool. Reduce oven temperature to 350°.

For Filling: Beat yolks. Pour in condensed milk, stirring constantly. Add lime juice and rind. Pour into crust and bake for 15 minutes at 350°. When the pie is cool, thinly slice 2 or 3 kiwi to decorate top of pie.

Looking for love in all the wrong places, Necee Regis ended up in the kitchen, running her own catering business, not because she didn't love art more than cooking. She started catering while a graduate student at the Mass College of Art, and opened her own business two years after receiving her MFA. "I didn't mean to stay in the food business, but when university teaching jobs were too difficult to find, I stuck with what I knew. Food and service." As a cook, she is imaginative and efficient and serene, imposing some emotional tribute for the ritual she seems to perform for a fee. Her friends have a stake in keeping her in the kitchen and out of the studio and gallery, and she returns the compliment by saying, "If I had my choice I'd only be in the kitchen cooking for friends."

Until that time, she's juggling careers. She exhibits her sculpture regularly in the Boston area, and in the summer she shows at the Group Gallery and teaches at Castle Hill. She makes dark moons of paper, embedded with sharp fragments of glass or mirror, so that they glitter like the shine on soft coal. Since we cannot see around to the dark side of the moon, there is no need for a back, and the moons are cut in half so that they may be hung on the wall. Often she exhibits them as wall installations, placed at eye level and beyond, high enough to be out of the reach of small children, one of whom strained to reach it, saying he wanted to feel the pillow.

Recently Regis married Louis Postel, the former publisher of *Provincetown Poets* and *Provincetown Magazine*, not to be confused with the current magazine of that latter name. Provincetown legend has it that Louis once appeared on stage under the spell of a stage hypnotist, who told Louis that he lived on the moon and was a moon person, and who therefore didn't speak English, but spoke Moon talk. The hypnotist hypnotised someone else who could translate Moon talk into English. The translator asked Louis, "What part of the moon do you come from, the light side or the dark side?" Louis answered, lucidly, "I come from the light side, but it's near the border."

Juggling two careers and a man after her own heart takes artistry, as

Regis concurs, "Most artists I know are also good cooks. I think it's because we think of food not only in terms of flavor, but also color, shape and texture. I know I do. I'll look at a dish and think, 'This needs something red,' and then I'll search my memory for the perfect red solution. I go through a not dissimilar process in the studio, selecting from my pile of debris the objects I need to embed in my paper surfaces."

Roasted Red Pepper Dip

1 large can (14 oz.)
    roasted red peppers
⅓ cup capers
1 oz. anchovy fillets
2 tablespoons extra virgin
    olive oil
2 tablespoons lemon juice
½ cup fresh parsley leaves

Rinse the peppers and capers in cold water and drain well. Put everything in a food processor and blend with short pulses until well mixed and chunky. Do not over process. Add more lemon juice or olive oil or some of each, to taste. Serve with crackers, toast, or Tuscan bread.

Irish Soda Bread or Soda Biscuits

3 cups all-purpose flour
pinch salt
½ cup sugar
pinch baking soda
3 level teaspoons
    baking powder
½ stick (4 oz.) unsalted
    butter, melted and cooled
1 egg, beaten
1 cup sour cream
¾ cup raisins
2 tablespoons caraway seeds,
    optional
unsalted butter, melted

Preheat the oven to 350°. Sift together the flour, salt, sugar, baking soda, and baking powder. Add the butter and egg to the flour mixture, followed by the sour cream, raisins, and caraway seeds. Stir until all the ingredients are mixed. Knead on a lightly floured surface for 2 minutes. Roll the dough into a ball. Place in a lightly greased 9-inch cake pan. Flatten slightly with the palm of the hand. Cut a shallow X across the top of the loaf. Bake 1 hour. Remove the bread from the oven and brush the top with melted, unsalted butter. For best results, eat this bread while it is still hot. Yields one loaf.

For biscuits: After kneading the dough, roll it out on a floured surface to a 1½-inch thickness. Cut out biscuits with a 1½-inch ring or biscuit cutter, and place them about 1 inch apart on lightly greased cookie sheets or jelly roll pans. Bake for 20 minutes at 350°. Remove the biscuits from the oven and brush the tops with unsalted butter while hot. Yields about 20 biscuits.

Artichoke-Mussel Sauce for Pasta

1½ cups white wine
1 garlic clove, crushed
10 sprigs parsley
3 dozen mussels
½ cup sun-dried tomatoes, sliced into thin strips
⅓ cup olive oil, approximately
1 or 2 garlic cloves, crushed
1 cup chopped onion
½ cup fresh parsley, chopped
1 can artichoke hearts, drained and lightly chopped
3 tablespoons fresh basil, chopped
½ teaspoon oregano
2 tablespoons extra virgin olive oil
salt and pepper to taste
1 pound spaghettini

Place the white wine, single garlic clove, whole parsley sprigs and mussels in a saucepan. Bring to a boil, then simmer until the mussels open. Strain the mussels and save the cooking juices. Remove the meats from the shells and reserve. Add the tomatoes to the mussel broth and set aside. (If the tomatoes seem very salty, rinse them in hot water before adding to the broth.)

Cover the bottom of a saute pan with about ⅓ cup olive oil. Add 1 or 2 crushed garlic cloves and the chopped onions. Saute on low heat until the onions become translucent, about 10 minutes. Add the chopped parsley, artichoke hearts, basil, oregano, and extra virgin olive oil. Stir until heated, about 2 or 3 minutes. Then add the tomatoes and mussel broth. Bring to a boil and simmer for 10 minutes. Just before serving, add the mussels and simmer until hot. Add salt and pepper. Ladle over spaghettini. Serves 2 to 4, depending.

"Sticks & Stones, 2," paper and wood

Chicken Liver Terrine with Sage and Juniper Berries

3 lbs. chicken livers,
  cleaned, fat removed
2 tablespoons dry sage
12 juniper berries
½ cup olive oil
1 garlic clove
1 cup dry red wine
8 oz. sweet butter, softened
  at room temperature
salt and white pepper
  to taste

Coarsely chop the chicken livers with the juniper berries. Heat the oil in a large heavy saucepan over medium heat. Add the livers, sage, and garlic. Saute for 10 minutes, stirring occasionally. Add the wine and cook for 10 minutes more. Remove the pan from the heat, strain excess liquid, and cool. Put the butter in a food processor and whip. Add the liver mixture and process until smooth. (Make sure it has cooled enough so it won't melt the butter.) Season with salt and white pepper. Spoon into an earthenware terrine or serving dish, seal with plastic wrap, and refrigerate. Remove from the refrigerator at least half an hour before serving. Serve with crackers or crusty bread. Makes 4 cups.

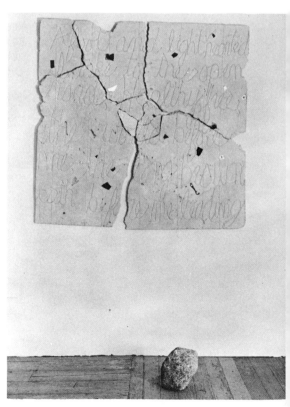

"Instant Archeology"
paper, hydrocal, debris and rock

MISCHA RICHTER

Renate Ponsold

Like most Russians, Mischa Richter takes his humor very seriously. He arrived in America early in the century when he was eleven years old, and soon, when he was old enough to suffer, he suffered the Depression, which taught him that "life is tragic, and if you think about it, you would slit your throat." Now in his seventies and living yearround in Provincetown, Richter continues as a staff cartoonist for *The New Yorker,* where his witty drawings appear regularly. They are the very model of *The New Yorker* cartoon, sophisticated and wryly critical, often choosing some topic in the art world as their topic. One cartoon, published in the inaugural issue of *Provincetown Arts,* shows a couple in an art gallery exclaiming over a painting with a price tag of $50,016.37: "Now there's an artist who knows the value of his work." The drawing would be amusing without the caption, and Richter is known for his ability to create cartoons that don't require explanation.

He believes that humor is a gentle criticism of life, while life is a savage criticism of humor. To be funny, he says, one must have thought deeply about issues just as a dramatist must, but a dramatist does not have the hard task of making people laugh. Richter says that he has seen a lot of dumb dramatists, but never a dumb humorist, because a humorist must make people laugh, while a dramatist has no immediate, audible test of success. For inspiration, he reads the Russian classics, currently Tolstoy's *Resurrection* and the poems of Pushkin, "heavy stuff," he says. He devotes other moments of the day to searching for something to chuckle about on daytime TV, finding it less funny than Pushkin but more hysterical than real life.

Depression Delicacy

1 lb. long grain rice,
  approximately, cooked
1 or 2 onions, chopped
1 or 2 green bell peppers,
  chopped
¼ lb. cooked ham, chopped
  into small pieces
olive oil
soy sauce to taste

Make enough rice to fill a large, deep frying pan. Cut up one or two onions, and one or two green peppers. Cut up ¼lb. of ham into small pieces. First, fry the onions in olive oil on a very slow fire. When onions are tender, add the pepper. When pepper is tender but not burned, pour the rice and ham in. Stir everything together. Add soy sauce and continue to cook slowly, adding olive oil if necessary. In about fifteen minutes, the dish will be ready to serve.

"Cut up one or two onions..."

Tomas Breuer

When not traveling on painting trips, most recently to the vistas of the far west, Helen Wilson returns to her Wellfleet home, taking special interest in tending the garden she uses to supply her summer kitchen. Winters she spends in New York in a Tribeca loft which she shares with the sculptor Timothy Woodman, whom she met over 18 years ago while a student at the Skowhegan School in Maine. Many of her paintings are started out-doors in a single day, then refined for months in her studio, with reference only to an intense memory of how she felt while there. "It's as if I were musical," she says, "with perfect pitch, and I went to somebody's house where they played something on the piano that was absolutely transfixing. If they played it for me several times, and I completely concentrated on it, I would remember it, both because I had the technical facility to memorize it and because I'd be so focused on it. I could then go home and play that piece for years, as long as I chose to remain connected to that memory."

Her works have a musical patterning in which shapes of exactly chosen colors echo kindred shapes in different colors. In one example, clouds drift in the distance while sky blue puddles of cloud-shaped water lay trapped in pockets of sand dunes, producing an eerie, levitating effect. Often she paints from great heights looking down. A sudden foreshortening occurs even in the angle of her miniature, "face-sized" landscapes, in which things seen far away occupy a scale equivalent to things seen close. A group of her paintings she calls "diary" paintings, since they make use of autobiographical moments. Occasionally they depict figures in rooms conversing importantly while small paintings line the walls, hanging with that slight misalignment that happens to paintings that have hung on a wall for many years. She paints mostly on Masonite panels, the paint applied very smoothly, producing a surface that is both hard and luminous, seemingly a compound of the momentary and the eternal. She says she wants to make paintings "from the heart, in which there is an image developed to the extent that there's a whole world inside it, with its own standards, where it has its own information, like a Rosetta Stone."

Born in Boston only because her parents, Edmund and Elena Wilson, wanted her to be born in a city hospital, Helen grew up largely in Wellfleet. The greatest luxury in her life, she says, is to have had "the scene of my youth be as resonantly beautiful as it was and still, now, to be able to enjoy it."

"From the Bluff," oil on masonite

Pea Soup with Mint

This recipe was invented by my mother.

1 cup water per person
1 package frozen peas per two people (fresh peas are wasted on this dish)
milk or cream
a handful of fresh mint, chopped
1 bouillon cube per 4 cups water, or salt to taste
plain yogurt

Bring the water to a boil and dissolve the bouillon cube in it (or add salt). Add pepper and the peas and cook them for as many minutes as the package directs. Put the peas and the liquid in a blender and puree. Return them to the pot and add the milk or cream and the mint. Heat, without boiling, and serve with a dollop of plain yogurt. This doesn't keep its color, which is bright green, if left in the refrigerator.

Fennel Fish for Two People

3 or 4 fillets of sole or
  flounder, depending on size
1 head of fennel (if it's more
  than the white bulb end,
  use only that bottom part)
1 tablespoon butter
  or margarine
1 tablespoon dried dill weed

Chop the fennel into pieces the size of pear blossoms and saute them in the butter or margarine until they become transparent or even a bit brown. (Use a flat pan big enough to take all the fillets lying flat at one time.) Add the dill and saute briefly; then remove the fennel to another dish while you cook the fillets in the same pan over low heat, adding extra butter if necessary, first one side, then the other. They cook very quickly; flip them before they cook too much on the first side so they don't fall apart. Shake the pan so the fillets don't stick. Spoon the fennel back over the fish and serve with a spatula immediately. The fillets are too delicate to transfer to a serving dish or to keep hot.

Jennifer's Ginger Idea

This is almost not a recipe, but it's a wonderful solution to dessert when you want something fancy and intense and you don't have the time to make it.

a jar of candied ginger
  in syrup
a pint of cream,
  the heavier the better

Serve each person two or three nuggets of the ginger with a wide streak of cream poured over them.

Renate Ponsold

Jim Forsberg has lived in Provincetown for over 30 years, arriving here on a bus with Lester Johnson one spring to look for a summer place. He liked the little white buildings, the sea and the smell. He turned to his traveling companion, a fellow artist, and said, "You know, I want to live here."

Forsberg was a self-described country boy from Sauk Centre, Minnesota, the town made emblematic of American provincialism in *Main Street* by Sinclair Lewis. Forsberg grew up wanting to be an actor, but after a scholarship year at the MacPhail School of Music and Drama in Minneapolis, he became convinced that his heart was not in acting, although to this day he continues to be active with the Provincetown Theater Company, appearing in plays such as *Enter a Free Man* and designing sets. At Christmas, in Sauk Centre, mulling things over, Forsberg, Swedish, taciturn and practical, made money by trimming store windows for the holiday, winning first, second and third prizes for his windows on Main Street.

He returned to Minneapolis to enter art school, transferring two years later to the St. Paul School of Art. During the war, he spent three years in the Pacific, having his first one-man show in the Red Cross lobby in Brisbane, Australia, in 1944, showing works done in tempera of action in New Guinea. On the G-I Bill, Forsberg went to the Art Student's League in New York, where his mentors included Cameron Booth, with whom he had studied while in St. Paul. One day in 1948 on a trip to the country north of New York City, Forsberg found himself on the property of his father-in-law, building a wall with large fieldstones. "As I was handling them, setting them in place," he recalls, "it occurred to me that you could make things with stones, or with the forms of stones."

For a seven-year period, following his first New York show at the Ashby Gallery, Forsberg began to work with stone-like shapes in his prints and paintings. The images are balanced one atop another, some cantilevered like the lintels that have sat for centuries at Stonehenge. "Everyone has a sense of balance, which you cannot defy. I want my stones to escape their weight, to be released from their physicality and achieve a luminous floating. I could cantilever something out there beyond where it would cease to tease you, where it would cease to work. I like precariously balanced forms, the feeling that there could be movement in the work and that the slightest little disturbance would upset the total order." Forsberg invented a novel technique for producing prints. Working with the woodblock, he impulsively glued matboard to the wood to save himself the trouble of cutting the wood away. "The whole resistance thing, which a sculptor just adores, was nothing to me," he explains. His stone prints were represented in important group shows, both nationally and internationally, including the Museum of Modern Art's "Young American Printmakers" in 1953.

Forsberg says that he keeps looking the word "abstract" up in the dictionary "because I keep forgetting what it means. I prefer the definition which talks about the ability to think in pure structures, without reference to actual signs. I translate that into an evocation of a thought process." His large paintings done in Provincetown utilize architectural structures such as portals and windows, becoming theatrical entrances and exits for a drama of rich colors. Loosely bundled in orbs which float chromatically, the blues drifting back, the yellows gliding forward, the colors press delicately against their frames like featherweight balloons.

Swedish Meat Balls

1 lb. ground round
½ lb. lean pork, ground
½ lb. veal, ground
4 slices wheat bread, crumbled
1 medium-sized onion, chopped, but not too fine
1 teaspoon salt
½ teaspoon ground nutmeg
1 teaspoon cardamom seeds, crushed
1 cup orange juice
2 eggs, beaten
1 pint sour cream
cornmeal
paprika

Grind the round, pork, and veal together with the bread. Add the onion, salt, cardamom, orange juice, and half of the ground nutmeg. Add the eggs and mix well with a wooden spoon. If the mixture is too wet, add small amounts of cornmeal to dry it out; if it is too dry, add small amounts of warm water. Make the meatballs by rolling a teaspoon of this mixture between the palms of your hands. (Dip hands in cornmeal before rolling the meatballs.) The meatballs should be about ¾-inch in diameter or one inch at most. Arrange on an oiled baking sheet and sprinkle with paprika. Brown in the oven at 350°. When the meatballs are done, take them from the oven and set them aside.

Make the sauce by mixing the sour cream and the remainder of the nutmeg with the pan drippings in a skillet over low heat. When the sauce is hot and well blended, remove the skillet from the heat. Put the sauce and the meatballs in a casserole, heat them together gently, and serve. These meatballs may be served cold, if desired.

Pancakes

⅔ cup all-purpose flour
⅓ cup cornmeal
1 heaping teaspoon baking powder
½ teaspoon baking soda
1 tablespoon yogurt
1 tablespoon sour cream
1 egg
salt to taste
oil

Mix the dry ingredients well. Add the yogurt, sour cream, and egg. Mix and beat by hand for thirty seconds.

Lightly oil a griddle or frying pan and heat on low. Test the heat by flicking cold water from your fingers onto the griddle. When the griddle spits back, it's ready. Pour or spoon small amounts of the mixture onto the griddle, sized to your liking. When bubbles begin to appear in the pancakes, flip them over and lightly brown the other side. Serve with soft butter and real maple syrup.

If the mixture is too stiff, add a small amount of cold water; if too thin, add a small amount of cornmeal.

For variations on this basic recipe, try adding bits of different flours to the original dry mixture; bran, oatmeal, or whole wheat are possibilities. Have fun experimenting.

Drawing

TABITHA VEVERS

Tabitha Vevers spent summers and pre-school years in Provincetown; winters she lived in Indiana, where her father taught art history at Purdue. After graduation from Yale University, a summer in Skowhegan, residency at MacDowell, a study trip to Italy, and a stint in Cambridge, she returned to live yearround in Provincetown. Represented by the David Brown Gallery in Provincetown and by the J. Noblett Gallery in California, her paintings sell with sufficient popularity to allow her to paint full time. Serving as a member of the Board of Trustees of the Provincetown Art Association and Museum, she has been the catalyst for a series of exhibitions ("Couples," "Words in Pictures," and "Tears and Laughter: A Show of Emotion") which have enlivened the off-season community with their interesting themes.

On her trip to Italy, she saw the frescos in Pompeii, with their scenes of daily life torn from the ancient walls, like little peaks through a curtain called Time. She began painting on cement fragments, simulating the antique effect, yet embedding it with paradoxes by pressing fossils of contemporary life, such as toothbrushes and scissors, into the cement. "I like to use contemporary imagery," she says, "as though you were seeing it from the future looking back in time." Fascinated with the narrative quality of pre-Renaissance icons, rather than viewing them as religious symbols, she saw them as depicting lovingly the timeless themes of human life — "love, loss, fear and joy," she says. Most often in her recent paintings, her figures are nude. She says she has tried to do clothed figures, but "they always seem incredibly awkward because they become a specific type of person instead of a specific feeling." To remove the images from a strictly modern context, she has been situating her narratives within architectural and theatrical frames — stage-like arches, temples, columns and pediments. In "Love Unbound," reproduced here, lovers leap from the splayed pages of a storybook, across the page division, as if the artist were rewriting the story, freeing the characters from an old story already told. (A pencil, sharpened and complete with eraser, rests on the bottom ledge of the frame, implying this revision.)

In an unusual father-daughter interview published in *Provincetown Arts*, Vevers observes that a painting of her father's, "Iphigenia," inspired her to write a poem called "Lone Stepper Marking Sand." The painting shows a young woman, perhaps fleeing, perhaps sprawled face down on the ground. The image is surrounded by numerous soles of old shoes found on Provincetown beaches by her father. The soles are worn, weathered, and embedded in dark sand, perhaps much as they appeared when they were first found. Resonant with associations, the soles suggest the sacrifice of the female heroine, Iphigenia, who becomes a victim of destiny in the Greek assault on Troy. Imagining her father's working process, Tabitha tells him, "I had this image of you walking along the beach, not only picking up soles, but leaving footprints behind." The soles which had once been worn by other people become emblematic of the human soul, in an ongoing evolution that would be lost but for the activity of the artist. If Tabitha Vevers's art is Veversesque, it is because, as she learned at Yale, "most of the people studying art were reacting *against* something, while I was going *with* something."

"Love Unbound," oil and acrylic on wood

Plein-Air Oysters on the Half Shell

I enjoy fresh ingredients simply prepared. Cooking is most rewarding to me when I have time to savor the whole process. On a winter's day in Provincetown, going out to dig clams is a pleasurable part of preparing a meal. For the $5 cost of a shellfish license, plus a good rake, you can bring home a bucket of cherrystones, quahogs, sea clams, steamers, oysters, or mussels. Below are two of my favorite recipes, to be enjoyed while your skin is still flushed from the winter sun and fresh air.

1 lemon
a pepper mill
a sharp knife
oysters or cherrystones

Bring a lemon, a pepper grinder, and a sharp knife out onto the sand flats with you. When you come across an oyster (or a cherrystone), open it by inserting the knife into the hinge and then cutting your way around the edge of the shell. Squeeze a slice of lemon onto the oyster, grind on a bit of pepper, and enjoy. You can't get them any fresher than that.

Clam Chowder

2 dozen quahogs (about), scrubbed
1 onion, diced
2 stalks celery, thinly sliced
1 or 2 tablespoons bacon fat, or a mixture of butter and oil
2 tablespoons flour
2 large potatoes, diced
3 cups milk, heated but not boiling
butter
freshly ground pepper

Place the quahogs in a large covered pot with 3 cups of water and simmer until all the clams are steamed open. Reserve one cup of the broth and mince the clams.

Saute the onion and celery in a saucepan with the bacon fat. When the onion is soft and golden, stir in the flour and cook through gently. Slowly stir in the reserved clam broth, being careful to stop short of pouring in any sand that has settled at the bottom of the pot. Add the potatoes, and enough water to cover. Cover the pot and simmer until the potatoes are done. Add the clams, then stir in the milk and simmer for five minutes. Do not allow the chowder to boil, as the milk will curdle and the clams will be tough. (Speaking from experience, the chowder will still taste good; it just won't look great.) Serve hot, topped with a knob of butter and freshly ground black pepper.

John Kearney is best known as the creator of a species of sculpture fabricated from chrome automobile bumpers. To make a goat weighing a hundred pounds, he must begin with half a ton of bumpers. He uses only the curved ends, removing them with an acetylene torch, a reduction process requiring increasingly difficult salvage due to the trend toward thinner, unusable steel as well as the introduction of rubber car bumpers. Sympathetic toward endangered species, Kearney has welded his bumpers into the images of such beasts as the bison, Siberian tiger, snowy egret, and white rhinoceros. "Detroit Horsepower," purchased by the big four automakers for the collection of Detroit's Children's Museum, is an homage to a free-running horse, rare in the land of the highway. The commemorative appeal of his work has earned Kearney many commissions. In Wichita, the Chisolm Trail is honored with his armor-plated longhorn cattle. John D. Rockefeller IV has a Kearney deer nibbling grass on his estate, and Johnny Carson has a Kearney camel shining in the desert sun near his Palm Springs home.

During the winter months, Kearney lives in Chicago, where he is the director of a highly successful Contemporary Art Workshop, an organization he founded in 1949 to provide studios, exhibition space, workshops, programs, and lectures for emerging midwest artists. Summers he spends in Provincetown, working in his studio on Harry Kemp Way, named for the poet, Harry Kemp, who lived sometimes in a cottage nearby, sometimes in a shack on the dunes. When Harry died, after quoting long passages from Shakespeare during a drinking bout at the Beachcombers, Kearney decided to do a memorial bust. Although he has made three-dimensional welded portraits of other artists, such as Hondius, Sol Wilson, Richard Florsheim, Eddie Euler, and Raphael Soyer, Harry's was the only one he has done in silver, perhaps because he felt Harry's spirit was so endangered. ("Harry's death that night," recalls Kearney, "is a Provincetown legend, about the way the town priest struggled over the body to get it cremated as requested, after Harry had converted to Catholicism on his deathbed, knowing at the time that it was against Catholic law to be cremated.") The portrait, reproduced in this book, shows Harry and his whiskers as a ghostly mesh of silver wire, frankly skeletal, enduring eternity as the physical equivalent of his memory, like a piece of driftwood hollowed out and burnished by the wind and weather.

Portuguese Soup or Kale Soup

**1½ lbs. linguica sausage
(Portuguese or Spanish)
cut into ⅜-inch pieces**
**¾ lb. dried kidney beans,
uncooked**
**¼ lb. dried white beans,
uncooked**
**1 large potato, cut into
small cubes**
**1 large onion, cut into
small pieces**
**1 or 2 tomatoes, chopped
(optional)**
**2 10-oz. packages frozen kale
or 1 lb. fresh kale, chopped**
**4 or 5 leaves fresh mint or
1 teaspoon dried mint**
water to cover

Soak the kidney and the white beans
overnight, then cook them until tender in
fresh water. Cut up the sausage and
saute it lightly in a large soup cauldron.
Add all the other ingredients (except the
kale) and cook until tender; then add the
kale. Add enough water to make it soup-
like; but as this is more a stew than a
soup, don't add too much, just a little
more than is necessary to cover all the
ingredients. Cook the soup for several
hours and then add the mint leaves. This
soup improves with age and makes a
hearty peasant-type meal. Good with a
bottle of red wine and crusty Portuguese
bread.

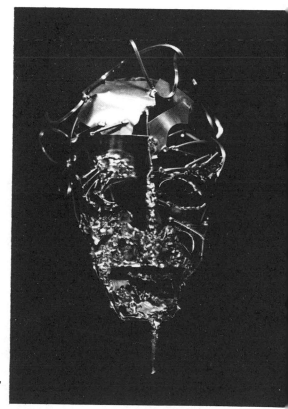

*"Portrait of
Harry Kemp"
Silver*

Chicken Naranja

1 frying chicken (3½ lbs.)
   cut into serving pieces
½ cup butter
½ cup slivered almonds
½ cup raisins
2 cups orange juice
   (you may want to cut this
   down to 1½ cups)
½ teaspoon cinnamon
¼ teaspoon ground cloves
¼ teaspoon nutmeg
1 orange, cut into
   ¼-inch slices
1 tablespoon flour mixed
   with 2 tablespoons water
   (for thickening)

This is a Mexican recipe.

Brown the chicken in butter in a large saucepan until it is golden. Mix the orange juice, cinnamon, cloves, nutmeg, and raisins so the spices are thoroughly blended. Pour this mixture over the chicken, cover the pan, and simmer on low heat for 40 to 50 minutes, or until the chicken is tender. During the last 15 minutes of cooking, add the almonds and the orange slices. When the chicken is done, thicken the pan juices with flour and cook for a few more minutes until the sauce has thickened. Serve over rice.

"Deer"
Bronze

Moussaka

1½ lbs. potatoes
olive oil for frying
2 medium onions, chopped
1 lb. very lean
  ground beef
2 garlic cloves, minced
1 8-oz. can tomato sauce
1 teaspoon cinnamon
salt and pepper
2 eggs
1 cup milk
⅓ cup Kefalotyri or
  Parmesan cheese

Preheat the oven to 350°. Peel the potatoes and cut them into ¼-inch slices. Fry these in hot olive oil until they are golden brown, and drain. Arrange half of the potatoes in an even layer in a shallow 1½-quart baking dish (or a 9-inch square pan). Saute the onion in olive oil until soft, and set aside. In the remaining oil, cook the meat until all redness disappears. Add the onion, garlic, tomato sauce, cinnamon, and salt and pepper and mix in. Pour the meat mixture over the first layer of potatoes and arrange the remaining potatoes on top. Beat the eggs, add the grated cheese, and combine with the milk. Pour this mixture over the potatoes and meat. Bake the casserole in the oven for 45 minutes. Cut it into squares to serve. Sprinkle with more grated cheese.

This can also be made with sliced zucchini or eggplant instead of potatoes.

Pat de Groot began to draw in 1964 after the death of her husband, the artist Nanno de Groot. In 1976 she ceased working as a book and book jacket designer for New York publishers, devoting full time to drawing.

Her drawings have a spare eloquence, showing the flap of a wing or a turn of the neck, rendered with minimal strokes. Most often, she uses a sharpened bamboo stick dipped in India ink. To make her drawings, she must work while in direct visual contact with the birds. "I take my energy from the birds," she admits. "It's almost a crutch. If it's not in front of me, I can't draw it." She uses her kayak to paddle to a rookery at Long Point. If the cormorants are roosting on the breakwater, she will bob in the water close by the rocks, her legs stretched awkwardly forward in the kayak, drawing on her lap. "I'll hit an hour or two when my hand works and the line is okay. The birds and the water come into the hand and onto the paper. My hand has to make the drawing and I have to find out how not to stop it because the bird is there and the water is there and somehow it comes through without interference from here," she says, pointing to her head.

Each summer she exhibits a selection of her drawings at the Provincetown Group Gallery, now located above the Tennis Club in an airy, high-ceilinged room. Recently she has made impressive installations by abutting over a hundred drawings along an expansive wall. "They fit together in the order I draw them and they make a large piece of work that has a rhythm of its own." From a distance the repetitions read like hieroglyphics, and she finds she is less interested in the single drawing than in what happens with many drawings. She adds, "I want my work to have the look of writing on the wall."

As a young woman, Pat de Groot found herself in Paris typing sections of Samuel Beckett for an early number of *The Paris Review*. One section, a 10-page paragraph, involved the proper sequential sucking of 16 stones, the character obliged "to move these stones in and out of his pockets and his mouth, working on a complicated logistic with the order of sucking each stone and where to put it after it has been sucked so it won't get sucked again before all 16 stones have, in turn, been sucked and put in the proper pocket."

Like Beckett's character, de Groot's birds repeat stylized postures until they transcend their absurdity. She has written, "I am looking to put down something about the way it is outside my windows. The way it is with the birds and the water. To find some bird intimacy. To draw a cormorant with its spirit intact. I want its weirdness, its archaic peculiarity to come through as recognizable so you too can see that this is a relative of yours you might not have noticed before."

Broiled Haddock or Scrod

Serves one:
1 large fillet of haddock
 or scrod
mayonnaise
1 red onion, finely chopped
4 mushrooms, chopped
corn meal
paprika, hot or sweet

Place the fish in a large, shallow pan, lightly oiled (or line it with foil if you don't want to wash the pan). Lightly spread mayonnaise over the fish with the back of a spoon. Cover the fish with the chopped onion. Sprinkle the mushrooms, diced fairly small, on top. Sprinkle some corn meal on top of that. Add a light shaking of hot or plain paprika. Broil three inches from the flame until the fish is just opaque. Serve with lemon.

Quick Squid Stew

There are small local squid available in the spring and early summer, and large-bone squid in late August and September. They are equally good fresh or frozen. To freeze, put them in a large freezer bag, four to a bag, as close to alive as possible. Press the air out of the bag. Zip lock and freeze without cleaning.

4 squid
1 large onion, chopped
1 block tofu
1 tablespoon tamari
1 green pepper, chopped
Oriental hot pepper paste
  (Kimchee is good)
2 crushed dry cayenne
  peppers
  or **1 fresh hot pepper,**
  chopped fine
½ cup mushrooms or
  scallions, chopped
  (optional)
parsley, chopped

To clean squid: Thaw. Cut in front of the eye, removing the tentacles but leaving enough of a piece so that the tentacles hold together in a circle. Remove the mouth, a ball-like piece of cartilage right behind the tentacles. Cut a small piece off the end of the tail. Take a piece of paper towel, push back the body skin, and grab hold of the backbone. Pull. It will come out in one piece. Trim the fins close to the body. Take a knife and insert it behind the head, cutting the entrails loose from the body top and bottom. Pull out and discard, or give them to the cat.

Run water through the body to clean. Scrape off any gook left inside. Slice the body, making rings about ¼-inch or less wide. Pat them dry, along with the tentacles and the tail fins.

In a large heavy skillet, lightly brown the cut-up onion in oil. Add cayenne pepper. In another small skillet, brown a few pieces of onion in oil. Cut the tofu into ½-inch cubes and let it cook with the onions in the small skillet until lightly browned on both sides. Add the tamari. Sizzle, then turn off the heat. To the onions cooking in the large skillet, add the cut-up green pepper. Turn up the heat. Add the squid. Stir until the squid becomes opaque — one or two minutes. Add half a cup of water. Then add one teaspoon of Oriental hot pepper paste. If you don't have this, substitute an available pepper sauce. Add the tofu. Don't make it too hot to eat. Cover and cook for a few minutes on medium heat. Add cut-up mushrooms at the last minute if you like, and scallions. Serve with brown rice and sprinkle with chopped parsley. Serves 4.

Chocolate Mousse

½ lb. bittersweet chocolate, best quality, made with vanilla, not vanillin
¼ cup strong black coffee
¼ to ½ cup terbinado or white sugar
5 eggs, separated
1 teaspoon vanilla extract
heavy cream

Melt together in a double boiler the chocolate, the coffee, and whichever sugar you prefer. When this melts, stir until velvety smooth. Remove from the heat and place the pan in cold water to cool.

Beat the egg yolks until creamy in texture and color; they should become very light yellow. Take a full five minutes to do this. Add the vanilla extract to the beaten egg yolks. Add this to chocolate mixture and fold in. Beat the egg whites until they make points. Fold them gently but thoroughly into the chocolate and egg yolk mixture. Pour into separate mousse pots and place in the refrigerator. They should set up quite firm. Serve the next day, topped with heavy cream.

Cranberry Preserves

2 quarts fresh cranberries
1½ cups apple cider
½ cup orange marmalade
½ cup light honey

Take about two quarts of large, local, ripe, wine-colored cranberries. They are riper and sweeter when you pick them in November. Put them in a pot. Pour about 1½ cups of apple cider over them. If the cider comes up to the second joint of your index finger, that should be enough. Put on high heat and bring to a boil. Let boil for a couple of minutes, covered—but most of the cranberries should stay whole. Turn off the heat. Add the orange marmalade (Dundee preferred) and the honey. Cool and put in jars.

James Hansen, Myriam LaPlante and Claude Simard will be remembered in Provincetown even if they never return to Provincetown. Living together on the compound of the Fine Arts Work Center during the summer of '84, the three shared studio space and participated in collaborative painting sessions. One called "Trilemma" consisted of three artists' solutions to the same dilemma of how to cover the interior of Duffy's studio at 211½ Bradford Street in a coherent overall style. As collaborators, their solution was to paint like each other, each bringing his or her own aspect to a communal neo-expressionism—"I'm the cerebral," LaPlante said, "James is the heart, and Claude is the impulsive." As part of a revised acquisition plan to purchase work by talented artists while they are living in Provincetown, the Art Association acquired examples of the work of each of them. The three continued to work collaboratively for several years, producing an 8000-sq. ft. mural for a church near Montreal and a 2500-sq. ft. installation of an epic narrative in an East Village gallery. Presently, LaPlante lives in Rome, and Hansen returns from Boston each summer to exhibit in Provincetown.

Jason Byron Gavan

Claude Simard shows regularly at the Jack Shainman Gallery in New York and Washington. His recent work consists of fewer figures in larger frames, wearing whitened faces afflicted charmingly with the woe of the world. Often they are dressed in the high collars and colorful costumes of Italian commedia dell'arte, where the sadness of the unrequited lover is a source of great amusement to his fellow comedians. A complex poignancy shines through the painted faces, the theatrical mask expressing hidden emotion, like the furrows in a clown's smile.

One of the many French Canadians who visit Provincetown the way Parisians visit the Cote d'Azur, Simard writes, "One summer I moved from Montreal to go on an adventure. I went to Provincetown because it had such a great reputation for its art and artists, even as far away as Montreal. When I arrived, I wasn't disappointed. I have always felt at home in Provincetown, never like an outsider. I met my great friend James Hansen there, and stayed through October in 1982, before I moved to New York. The next summer I returned with Myriam LaPlante, who had come down from Canada. The three of us were inseparable. Now we have all gone our separate ways."

Pasta al Basilico

36 fresh plum tomatoes
2 bunches fresh basil
5 garlic cloves
1 bunch parsley
2 cups extra virgin olive oil
salt and black pepper to taste
2 dried red peppers, chopped
½ cup white wine (optional)
1 lb. F.lli De Cecco pasta
Parmesan cheese,
    freshly grated

Boil the tomatoes whole, until the skins are easily removed, and remove the skins. Finely chop the garlic and parsley together. Place the garlic and the parsley in a 9-inch pot with ¼ cup olive oil and the crushed red pepper. Cook over low heat, stirring constantly. When the garlic is golden, add the peeled tomatoes. Chop the basil coarsely and add it to the tomatoes gradually. Let simmer for 2 hours. At this point, add ½ cup white wine, if desired. After 2 hours, add the rest of the olive oil and let the sauce sit, without stirring, for one hour before serving.

Cook the pasta, drain, and return it to its pot. Add the sauce, Parmesan cheese, and salt and pepper to the pasta. Mix together and serve. Serves 8.

Tourtiere du Lac St. Jean

Pastry:
3 cups flour
2 teaspoons baking soda
1 cup shortening
1 cup cold water

Mix the flour and baking soda together. Cut in the shortening. Add the cold water and mix well. Cover the dough and chill it for 30 minutes to an hour.

(continued on following page)

Filling:

1 lb. pork, cut into
½-inch cubes
1 lb. veal, cubed
1 lb. beef, cubed
1 hare, chopped
(use the head)
8 cups potatoes, cubed
1 can beef broth
2 onions, chopped
salt and pepper
water

Season the meat, and stir all the ingredients together in a big bowl. Roll out ⅔ of the pastry and place it in a large casserole dish. Turn the meat mixture into the casserole and add water to cover. Roll out the remaining pastry and cover the casserole with it. Pinch the edges together and poke holes in the top so that it can breathe. Bake the *tourtiere* in the oven at 400° for 1 hour. Cover, and cook at 250° for 5 to 6 hours.

Sugar Pie

Pastry:

3 cups flour
2 teaspoons baking soda
1 cup shortening
1 cup cold water

Filling:

1½ cups brown sugar
1 tablespoon flour
10 oz. light cream

Mix the flour and baking soda together. Cut in the shortening. Add the cold water and mix well. Cover the dough and put it in the refrigerator for 30 minutes to an hour. Roll out and place in two 8- or 9-inch pie pans.

For the filling, mix the sugar, flour, and cream well. Pour into the two uncooked pie crusts. Bake at 350° for 25 to 30 minutes.

"Untitled," oil

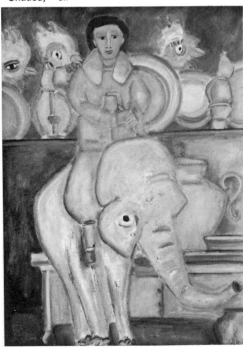

Moe Van Dereck is unique for the range of Provincetown experiences he has absorbed. He was an expert waiter at Ciro and Sal's in its early heyday, when it was frequented by many of the artists associated with the exciting Sun Gallery, a time when the restaurant had no time clock for its employees (most of them friends anyway) and when the long table tucked in the corner near the kitchen, called the "family table," usually had a portion of its bench free, a great place for the 63-second catnap while the cook hovered over the boiling water ready to pull the spaghetti. Amid Italian chaos, Moe was calm as a rock in a Zen garden, rising exactly as the cook was spooning the red sauce over the pasta, Often, after hours at Ciro's or at the nearby Beachcombers, Moe played guitar at a spontaneous party. For many years he has performed with the Surf Club's Jug Band. He was a Fellow at the Fine Arts Work Center the first year it was formed, and, as an artist, he continues to utilize materials which he has come to know through his parallel career as a carpenter and bulkhead builder, fashioning sculpture from wire, nails, even tools. On Saturday nights, usually after a session of three-cushion billiards with Conrad Malicoat, Moe presides as Skipper over the meetings of the Beachcombers. In addition, on Tuesday nights at his brother Napi's Restaurant, he plays chess with the chess club he organized, sharing gossip about the strange case of Bobby Fischer, former world champion who now rides the buses in Los Angeles waiting for someone with a soul to write a song about him.

Simie Maryles, married to Moe, has adapted her food habits to suit a "landscape painter on the go, or any person living in the fast lane, who must

Moe Van Dereck with son Joshua

Simie Maryles with new son Orion

refuel the body while they stay moving." She advises, "If you ride your bike out to your painting location you can pack seeds and raisins in small plastic jars (not glass, which can break) and eat with one hand as you steer with the other. You will never have to stop at all till you get where you want to go.

"Until they invent a pill called 'Lunch,' peanut butter and butter on wheat bread makes a good sandwich. Don't neglect to add the butter, or you'll never get your mouth unglued. The old PB&J standby, I find too sweet and yucky. Cut the sandwich into four pieces and you can manage it fine in a car or on a bike. You can drink coffee truck-driver style, with a small tear in the top, and hardly spill any. I don't know if anyone would call this cuisine, but it keeps some of us alive. If you reach the point of taste-bud boredom, take the day off from painting and go out for a real lunch."

She began her career painting rapid street portraits in places such as the huge flea market in Englishtown, New Jersey. For many years she did over 150 portraits a year, "Until I OD'd," she says. "Now I hardly do any, though something invisible creeps in when I put figures in my landscapes and the painting has something to do with people. I found there was a lot of theater and psychology in portrait work, and after I got my hand to stop shaking in public, I found that the way to support the art was to become the art. If I do portraits now, I'd like them to say something about the person." Her work has been particularly well received in California, where it has sold out at the openings of three successive one-person shows at a Pasadena gallery, inspiring the gallery recently to take out a full page color ad in *Artforum* of a pastel, "Pamet River Reflections." A local reviewer wrote, "The artist's vision is so peaceful and serene, it is difficult to avoid being captured by the relaxed atmosphere. To view is to let your blood pressure drop and your mind wander. The brilliant autumn reds combined with the pastoral setting are unapologetically seductive."

Simie Maryles, pastel

Fast Fish Chowder

1 large onion, chopped
1 oz. butter
2 potatoes, diced
1 lb. firm-fleshed white fish
   such as cod or haddock
salt pork
corn oil
½ quart milk, approximately
salt to taste

Saute the onions in butter until soft. Boil the potatoes, which have been cut up into fairly small pieces, to a point just short of being soft (*al dente*). Cut up the fish into bite-size pieces and cook it, in just enough water to cover, to a point just short of falling apart.

In a large soup pan, brown to a crisp some small chopped up pieces of salt pork in a small amount of corn oil. Add the cooked fish along with the water it was cooked in..Add the drained cooked potatoes and the sauteed onions. Add some milk to obtain a nice balance of liquid and solid. Heat the chowder to just short of boiling and simmer it for an hour. Only add salt to taste.
Serves 4 to 6.

For variety, add a can of cooked tomatoes and some hot pepper to the chowder.

Chicken and Broccoli Stir-Fry

2 cups chicken, cut into
   small pieces
peanut oil for stir-frying
pinch of garlic powder
4 tablespoons tamari
   soy sauce
½ cup onions, sliced
   lengthwise
1 cup fresh mushrooms,
   sliced
3 cups thin-sliced broccoli
   (sliced against the grain,
   with a diagonal motion)
½ cup spring water,
   approximately
2 tablespoons cornstarch
slivered almonds

Pour a little peanut oil into a wok, sprinkle in the garlic powder, and add the chicken. Cook on high flame, stirring with a wooden spoon, until the chicken turns white. Add the soy sauce and cook for another minute or two. Remove the chicken from the wok and set aside.

Place the sliced onions and a few drops more of peanut oil in the wok. Cook for a few minutes; then add the mushrooms and the broccoli. Add about ½ cup spring water. Cover the wok and steam the contents for three or so minutes. Return the chicken to the wok and stir into the vegetables. Make a mixture of cornstarch and water. Add this, stirring all the while, until the sauce thickens. Toss in some slivered almonds and serve immediately over Brown River rice (short grain is my favorite)—and that's it. Serves 4.

**1 whole fresh fish, gutted
butter for frying
paprika**

Skin and bone the fish. (Be sure to get a fish with a head and a tail so that you can enjoy skinning and boning it.) Get the skin off first. Start peeling it next to the tail, and with pliers pull it off toward the head. Now bone the fish by slicing from the tail toward the head with a sharp knife. (As you can see, there is no need to scale a fish you've skinned.) If you run into lots of nasty little bones that you can't seem to get rid of, try another kind of fish.

Rinse the fish off with water and dry it a bit. Now melt some butter in a non-stick frying pan. Put in the fish, and be sure not to burn it by having the flame too high. Carefully watch the sides of the cooking fish, and the moment you see that they are changing color (looking cooked, opaque), quickly slip the fish over and cook it for the same amount of time as on the first side.

Sprinkle with paprika. This brings out the flavor and shows by the way it's applied just how artistic the cook really is.

Serve the fish with fresh cut lemon wedges and fresh parsley.

*Moe Van Dereck
"Eastern Washerwing"
metal sculpture*

For the past 12 years Jackson Lambert has written a column for the *Advocate* called "Jackson Hole," a chronicle of bar conversations based on regulars of the old Foc's'le, no longer in existence. Like characters from Pirandello's play, *Six Characters in Search of an Author,* Lambert's people exist in a dreamy limbo, in which the life they are living is not yet shaped into a work of art. Always looking for a fast buck and a quick shot of Jim Beam, they talk a kind of punning double-talk in which nonsense is twisted to make a kind of sense, their wisdom redeeming some lost aspect of their lives.

In his own life, Lambert has cultivated both Dionysus and Apollo. He was impulsive enough to fall in love with his wife at first sight when he was a soldier during the war and Carmen worked in the Army art department. After a brief courtship they wisely did not see each other for nine years, Carmen going to Japan and Jackson working as the art director of an ad agency in Washington. On a visit, following a blood test, they married, recruiting for their witness a man wandering in the hallway of the courthouse wearing a nice hat.

Lambert first became acquainted with Provincetown through LaForce Bailey, his art professor at the University of Illinois who summered in Provincetown. Staying a winter in 1941, Lambert remembers bartending at Mac's Bar when the regulars, John Dos Passos, Bruce McKain, and Harry Kemp, were almost the only customers. The novelist, the painter, and the tramp poet spent many evenings together. Dos Passos, wearing a tattersall vest, a tie, and a golfing cap, would discourse on writing while Lambert poured whisky, absorbing lessons about fiction and social commentary. McKain heard Lambert's confession that he was afraid of the colors yellow and white, and Harry Kemp sat sipping white port never dreaming that a Provincetown street would be named after him.

For this cookbook, Lambert has contributed the following explanation of how an original dish like "tacoweenies" gets created. He writes, "One of the favorite native indoor winter sports in Provincetown is fantasizing summer business enterprises that will net one a zillion from the tourists. Artists are little prone to these streetwalker's nightmares, but they can get snared up in them, as one day when our friend Ralph came over all steamed up over a rare opportunity offered him to operate a hot dog stand down on Lopes Square. Mexican food was then just beginning to drift up here from El Paso, so Ralph planned, in addition to the hot dogs and clam fare, to serve tacos, buritos, nachos and enchiladas. What Ralph needed from us was to delve down into the cesspool of our advertising experience and come up with a catchy business name. That was easy: Tacoweenies! Lean, clean, mean, all-American, and Ralph didn't like it. Too quick it was, for Ralph's ponderous thinking: anything easy was a sin. So he named his grease pit something like: 'Ralph & Madge's Lower Cape Yankee & Mexican Finger Food Emporium.' They made a bundle and dropped us as friends, and that's how things go around here.''

Tacoweenies

Refried beans:
4 onions, diced
lard
3 cans pinto beans
1 lb. mozzarella, sliced
1 teaspoon cumin

Chile rellenos:
4 cans whole green chiles
1 cup Cheddar cheese, grated
2 eggs
2 tablespoons butter
ripe olives,
**   sliced (for garnish)**
1 lb. hot dogs
shredded lettuce, diced
**   onions and grated**
**   Cheddar cheese**
tortillas, allow 2 per person

To make the refried beans: saute three large Texas onions in lard, add the pinto beans, sliced mozzarella, and 1 teaspoon cumin. Mix together and mash beans.

To make the chile rellenos: stuff the green chiles with wedges of Cheddar cheese. Beat the eggs with two tablespoons of warm water, and batter the chiles in this. Saute the rellenos gently in butter on both sides until browned. Garnish with sliced ripe olives.

To prepare the tortillas: line the bottom of a folded warm tortilla with refried beans, top with a boiled hot dog, and pile on lettuce, diced onions, and grated Cheddar cheese. Top with chile sauce and wash it down with Dos Equis or Corona beer if you are out of tequila.

Squid Pie

1 **dozen medium-sized local squid**
2 **cups diced potatoes, approximately**
1 **cup chopped onion, approximately**
2 **garlic cloves, crushed**
1 **can tomatoes**
red wine
dash Worcestershire sauce
2 **tablespoons olive oil**
1 **teaspoon allspice**
salt and pepper to taste
flour for thickening
pastry for a two-crust pie

*Refer to pages 36 or 105 for instructions on cleaning squid.

Clean the squid (this is an easy task; just ask anyone who has never done it),* and cut the flesh into ¾-inch squares and the tentacles into one-inch strands, saving the largest head entire. Put the squid, diced potatoes, onion, garlic, tomatoes, a shot of red wine, olive oil, allspice, salt and pepper, and Worcestershire sauce into a pan and boil for 25 minutes. You may have to add some water along the way. At the end, add some flour to thicken the combination. Line a deep pie dish with the pastry, put in the squid combo, cover with a top crust, and punch a few air holes in it. Take the set-aside squid head, embed it firmly in the center of the top crust, as illustrated, and bake until the crust is well browned and the exposed head is tender. If this were a Portuguese dish, it might be called *Lula Torta*.

HOW ABOUT...

From "Souvenir of Provincetown," art and copy by Jackson Lambert, published by Napi Van Dereck Press, Provincetown, Mass.

MR. TURNER
PAINTS HIS FIRST NUDE

FRANZ MARC GETS THE IDEA
FOR THE BLUE RIDERS

FRANCISCO JOSE DE GOYA
DOES HIS MAJA

FRANZ KLINE
FISHES FOR A COMPLIMENT
FROM DE KOONING

DOLLY SALVADOR
DOES HER FIRST
BUM BEARDSLEY

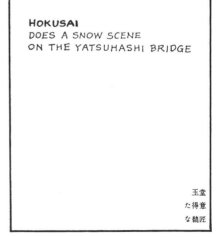

HOKUSAI
DOES A SNOW SCENE
ON THE YATSUHASHI BRIDGE

玉堂
た得意
な鵜匠

Murray Zimiles was five years old when he escaped Brooklyn and spent his first summer in Provincetown, living in a small shack on the dunes with his artist-uncle, Boris Margo. Tagging along on searches for beach salvage, under the big skies of the deserted back shore, little Murray was told to "look down" so that he would not miss any finds. Driftwood had at least three uses: to build and repair the shack they lived in, to contribute to the vocabulary of shapes used in Margo's painting, and to burn as firewood. Zimiles remembers "gathering up driftwood and helping Boris construct huge sculptures which served as the bonfire centerpieces for his annual 'August full of the moon' parties. These were enormous gatherings of hundreds of people who came to the back shore to dance, sing, read poetry, and, as the night wore on, engage in other bacchanalian activities. Boris enlivened these parties with his recitation of the poetry of Mayakovsky and demonstration of a singing voice that could break glass."

In his subsequent career as an artist, Zimiles has focused on the ecstatic image. Moments of revelation are expressed through impassioned postures of men, women, and mythological beasts. Nostrils flare and bodies surge with adrenalin. Horses stampede over their own shadows. Recurrent themes concern Genesis, the expulsion of Adam and Eve from Paradise, the

Holocaust, the artist as creator in his studio, and the artist as naked beast. As the Tahitians said of Gauguin, Zimiles too is the "man who makes men." Often figuring with objective narcissism as the subject of his own work, Zimiles is amazed by the divine power of the artist to fashion images in his own likeness. He works in several mixed media, oil, graphite, cast paper and printmaking, combining and blurring the same figure so that it appears staggered between separate temporal moments, as in the motion studies of the photographer Eadweard Muybridge.

Zimiles keeps wild his long red-blond hair and full beard. Less scrawny than wiry, he often presents himself naked, along with the likeness of his female mate. He writes, "needless to say, Martha is the major cook in our family so it is fitting that she be part of this. You can bill her as the designer-weaver."

Ragout for the Mayor's Female Relations

When we were living in a small (population: 250) southern French town that was defiantly and proudly communist, we became friends with the mayor, a young plumber who was in love with one of our students. The prevailing wisdom was, of course, that Americans knew nothing of cuisine, no matter how that was defined, and God forbid that any one of them should cook for you. These prejudices found some support in the example of one of our students, who lugged a ketchup bottle to every meal and dumped it hungrily on whatever. Since the mayor, who lived with his mother, sister, and aunt, had been so kind and welcoming to our small art school; and since he had treated us to a wonderful meal and experience in a small restaurant in the mountains, full of Provencal-speaking shepherds and their homemade cheese, I took up the culinary challenge and invited him to a meal, offering the following rabbit recipe (my own). He was very polite and gracious, but when he spied the likes of prunes and raisins in his stew, he made a generalization about the odd habit of the English of combining sweet with meat. The meaning of a reference to English cooking by a Frenchman was not lost on me. The end of the evening found him taking the entire pot (and its remaining contents) down the little unpaved alley to his female relations like some sort of trophy from an exotic country—after consuming three portions himself.

Martha Zimiles

good green olive oil
1 skinned rabbit, quartered
¼ cup green olives
¼ cup oil-cured black olives, Nicoise or Italian
¼ cup raisins or currants
12 large pitted prunes
Herbes de Provence (rosemary, thyme, a little sage, bay leaf)
6 to 10 garlic cloves, peeled and smashed
2 or 3 onions, chopped
2 tablespoons flour
1 cup dry white wine
½ cup water or stock
1 large cast-iron pot with lid

Saute the meat pieces in olive oil in the pot. When lightly browned, remove from the pot and set aside. Saute the onions and garlic gently. Stir in the flour and cook it a little. Deglaze with the wine and stock. Add the fruits, herbs, and meat.

Cook the ragout in the oven, covered, at 350°, until done. Turn the pieces and stir once after about 30 minutes of cooking.

Baked Banana Flambe
with Essence of Apple Cider

1 banana per person
butter
apple cider
Cognac

To make the essence of cider: Freeze the fresh apple cider. Allow it to defrost. The thick liquid that defrosts first is the syrupy essence.

The flambe: Slice the bananas lengthwise. Saute in butter until they are lightly brown on both sides. Place them in an oven dish with the essence of cider poured over the bananas. Baste as they bake for 15 minutes at 350°. Transfer to a serving dish. Pour Cognac over the bananas and ignite at the table, basting the bananas with the remaining Cognac/essence-of-cider mixture.

"Self Portrait,"
oil and graphite on paper

Susan Baker is the kind of artist who knows that cynicism is simply common sense. She attended the Rhode Island School of Design, briefly taught elementary school in Rhode Island, then moved to Provincetown, where she became a Fellow at the Fine Arts Work Center in 1969 during its first full year of existence. Baker claims she moved to Provincetown as a drop-out, knowing P-town by hearsay as a place where people came to get high or go crazy. Of course this was back in the '60s. Like many of the anonymous characters in Roger Skilling's chronicle of the low life of that period, *P-town Stories, Or the Meatrack,* Baker lived a marginal existence, working summers as a waitress, where she learned that "regulars" means "regular pains in the ass." If she was not exactly smiling as she shouted orders across the counter of the Cafe Edwige, there was more than a residue of wit in her depictions of the figures she met, such as the "macro-neurotic" who won't have sugar or syrup on his buckwheat pancakes, who sits crosslegged in the booth while he chews each bite 25 times, and who, an hour and no tip later, lights up an unfiltered Camel and inhales deeply.

Baker turns such characters into papier-mache sculptures which can be as witty as the puppets of Red Grooms and yet as solemnly iconic as the cloth hamburgers of Claes Oldenburg. Usually painted bright clown colors, her satirical pieces are built without armatures on a core of outrage. To a black and yellow steel-belted tire, Baker has affixed a pair of breasts—because, she says, "anything will sell if you put breasts on it."

Married to a poet, Keith Althaus, who is also a former Fellow of the Fine Arts Work Center, Baker founded in 1984 the Susan Baker Memorial Museum, which she describes as "a gallery of humorous art." Located in the front rooms of their house in North Truro, the museum co-exists with life, and chairs may be a pedestal for a piece of sculpture or a place to sit. Shelves are lined with varying pieces of sculpture, with price tags dangling. T-shirts and postcards are displayed with her drawings, such as "MY MOM HAS AN ATTITUDE PROBLEM." The "museum" is her symbolic response to the marketing realities of achieving fame and fortune as an artist. In addition, she sells the half-dozen "artist's books" she has produced, some as Xeroxes, under such titles as *Thoughts of a Human, How to Criticize Art,* and *Dogs I Have Known.* Increasingly popular, the artist's book is a genre that Baker pioneered.

Although much of her work satirizes something autobiographical, from the birth of a child to a complaint of her husband, it receives Althaus's praise as "good fiction." Yet when it comes to food, she and he confess they carry on an adversarial relationship.

Stolen-From-The-New-York-Times-Chicken

2 tablespoons sesame oil
1 teaspoon grated ginger root
1 or 2 garlic cloves, crushed
2 cups cooked chicken, chopped
1 large onion, chopped
1 cup bok choy (Chinese cabbage) or green cabbage, chopped
1 cup spinach, washed and shredded
1 cup broccoli, chopped
oyster sauce, hoisin sauce, or plum sauce
¼ to ½ cup sherry
1 tablespoon cornstarch

Saute the ginger and garlic in the sesame oil in a hot wok for a few seconds.

Add the cooked chicken, chopped onions, chopped bok choy or green cabbage, spinach, broccoli, and anything else you want. Add some water.

Then add the oyster sauce, hoisin sauce and/or plum sauce to taste and let it cook with the cover on it until the vegetables are done. Stir sometimes.

Mix the sherry and cornstarch and add it, stirring constantly.

Serve over rice noodles or rice during the commercial break in "The People's Court." Serves 4.

Uncle Tom's Cold Noodles and Rosemary

noodles
broccoli
rosemary
1 can tuna, drained
mayonnaise, preferably
    homemade

Cook some noodles and some chopped broccoli in the same water. Drain them and add fresh rosemary, the tuna, and some mayonnaise. Mix well, chill, and serve.

THE PERFECT MATE
To MY STEEL—
BELTED RADIAL

DOUGLAS HUEBLER

Douglas Huebler is physically a large man, six feet four, 200 pounds plus, with a booming voice, a barrel chest, and three years as a Marine Corps sergeant during the thick of World War II. Today he is highly regarded as one of the pioneer Conceptual artists, involved with questioning the necessity of the art object's physical reality. He asks, "Is art, in essence, conceptual or perceptual?" He has made maps in which he declares dots to be the location of "appearance." He has photographed icicles melting and announced they were images of time. "The world is full of objects, more or less interesting," he says. "I do not wish to add any more."

In 1971 Huebler assigned himself the Herculean task of photographing the existence of everyone alive, a project in which a series of candid snapshots, usually made in public situations, is presented in conjunction with aphorisms making arbitrary claims, such as one that says, "REPRESENTED ABOVE IS AT LEAST ONE PERSON WHO MIGHT FEEL PLEASED TO HAVE BEEN MADE THE SUBJECT OF ART." Huebler's wit in destroying some of the traditional structures of art has a dimension of deconstructive sorrow, which he calls "crocodile tears," but which are actually brief fictions taking the form of comic strips, interviews, and statements. These stories lament the loss of representation in postmodern art. The work of art, in an age of mechanical and electronic reproduction, might be said to consist of images without originals. Recently, Huebler has gone so far as to present printed reproductions of acknowledged masterpieces by artists such as Degas, Leger and Mondrian, and through the fictional "Great Corrector," Eric Lord, pointing out how these works are flawed by poor drawing, color and composition. Alongside these "flawed" works, he presents a hand-painted "corrected" version, making us question if his original fake is more real than the photographically simulated original.

Huebler, who has taught at Harvard, recently retired as Art Program Director at Cal Arts. His work is in the collections of numerous museums, including the Museum of Modern Art, and he shows regularly in New York with Leo Castelli. Since 1963 he has been a summer resident of Truro, spending summers attempting to correct his flawed tennis. (He now intends to live on the Cape full-time with his wife, Stephani Weinschel, and two year old daughter, Kate.)

As a cook, he is modest, disclaiming credit for any originality. Regarding the recipes he contributed to this book, he writes, in a characteristic gesture of self-disappearance, "These recipes are really those of Pearl Heyman, my mother-in-law! My only original ideas—seriously—are sandwiches. Favorites: peanut butter with jelly and liverwurst or peanut butter with mayo and sliced onion. Please credit Mrs. Heyman for her creations, and mention me, if you like."

. . . he illustrates the value of the well trained eye by showing his audience reproductions of works of art flawed by poor drawing, color, composition etc., alongside of which he displays his version of how the work should look. Not even the greatest —

from "Crocodile Tears"

Hot Crab Spread Steffi

**8 oz. fresh crabmeat,
 cartilage removed
¼ cup lemon juice
3 oz. cream cheese
 at room temperature
1 tablespoon heavy cream
⅓ cup mayonnaise
1 tablespoon minced onion
1 tablespoon chopped chives
½ garlic clove, minced
salt to taste
dash hot pepper sauce
dash Worcestershire sauce**

Marinate the crabmeat in the lemon juice for one hour. Drain. Whip the cream cheese and cream until smooth. Beat in the mayonnaise, onion, chives, garlic, and salt. Blend well. Fold in the crabmeat and add the pepper and Worcestershire sauces. Transfer to a one quart heatproof dish and bake for 30 minutes at 350°. Serve with crackers or thinly sliced party rounds (rye or pumpernickel bread). Serves 10.

Pearl's Creation

This baked cheese dip is tantalizing. It can be served with raw vegetables or crackers and can be served either hot or cold. Credit my mother-in-law, Pearl Heyman for these recipes, excerpted from her soon-to-be-published family cookbook.

1 cup fresh Parmesan cheese
1 cup mayonnaise
1 6-oz. jar
  marinated artichokes
1 tablespoon grated onion
½ teaspoon lemon juice
salt and pepper to taste

Use a food processor or blender to grate the cheese: with the sharp metal blade of the processor, cut up the cheese until it looks granular, not too fine. Add mayonnaise and mix in. Drain most of the liquid from the artichokes and chop them coarsely. Add the onion and the artichokes to the mixture in the food processor, with the lemon juice and the seasoning (you don't need much). Process until reasonably smooth (the mixture will be a little grainy, and should be, to give it texture). Bake in a small casserole at 350° for 20 to 30 minutes, until slightly brown on top.

The freshly grated Parmesan is a must, because it gives the dip its unusual flavor.

Jambalaya

2½ to 3 lb. broiler-fryer
  chicken, quartered
¼ cup butter or margarine
4 sweet Italian sausages,
  halved crosswise (½ lb.)
1½ cups ham cubes, cut in
  1-inch cubes
1 cup sliced onions
1 green pepper, cut in
  1-inch squares
2 garlic cloves, crushed
1 teaspoon dried thyme
¼ teaspoon chili powder
1 can tomatoes (16 oz.)
1 can chicken broth
  (13¾ oz.)
1½ teaspoons salt
¼ teaspoon pepper
1 cup raw long-grain
  white rice
2 tablespoons chopped
  parsley

Wipe the chicken pieces with damp paper towels. In hot butter in a six-quart Dutch oven, brown the chicken, turning until golden-brown all over, 15 to 20 minutes. Remove the chicken. Saute the sausage in the drippings in pan, until browned all over. Remove. Add the ham cubes, and saute until browned. Remove. Preheat oven to 350⁰. To the same drippings, add the onion, green pepper, garlic, thyme, and chili powder; cook, stirring, about five minutes. Add the tomatoes, chicken broth, salt and pepper, and the rice; mix well. Add the chicken, sausage, and ham; stir to combine. Bring to a boil. Bake, covered, for one hour or until the chicken and rice are cooked and most of the liquid is absorbed.

You may serve this right from the pot, or transfer it to a large serving dish. Sprinkle with chopped parsley. Serves 6.

Apricot or Viennese Torte

This is a delicious recipe that tends to be time consuming to make, but I think it is well worth the effort. I make the cake the day before I serve it, and do not refrigerate it. I use toothpicks (about 8), standing them evenly on top of the cake; then I cover it with plastic wrap or foil, so it won't dry out.

Torte Shell:

1½ cups sifted flour
2 tablespoons sugar
1 teaspoon salt
½ cup corn oil
2 tablespoons cold milk
1 egg yolk
¼ cup apricot preserves
9 x 12 cake pan or a 10-inch
　spring-form pan

Sift the dry ingredients directly into the pan or spring-form pan. Combine the oil, milk, and egg yolk in a measuring cup. Whip with a fork and pour all at once over the flour mixture. Mix with a fork until the flour is completely dampened. Press this pastry dough evenly and firmly to line the bottom and up the sides of the pan to a height of two inches. Brush the entire shell with the apricot preserves. Set aside while preparing the cake. (I heat and strain the preserves before brushing the shell.)

Torte:

1⅓ cup sifted cake flour
⅔ cup sugar
1½ teaspoon baking powder
½ teaspoon salt
½ cup finely chopped,
　lightly toasted almonds
　(put on a Pyrex pie plate
　and place under the broiler
　for a few moments,
　watching carefully)
⅓ cup corn oil
2 egg yolks
½ cup milk
1 teaspoon almond extract
⅛ teaspoon cream of tartar
2 egg whites
¼ cup apricot preserves

For the cake, mix and sift together the cake flour, sugar, baking powder, and salt. Stir in the toasted almonds. Make a well and add, in order, the corn oil, egg yolks, milk, and almond extract. Beat until smooth. Add the cream of tartar to the egg whites. Beat until the whites form very stiff peaks. Gently fold the whites into the batter until well blended. Pour the mixture into the torte shell and bake in a 350° oven for 40 to 50 minutes. Cool for eight to 10 minutes on a cake rack, then remove from the pan. When the cake is thoroughly cool, cover the surface with ¼ cup apricot preserves. Using a pastry bag, decorate the top of cake with rosettes of apricot frosting (recipe follows).

Apricot Frosting:

1 egg white
⅓ cup apricot preserves
1 tablespoon sugar
¼ teaspoon almond extract

Beat the egg white and the preserves together until stiff. Gradually beat in the sugar and continue beating until very stiff peaks form. Blend in ¼ teaspoon almond extract. Use to decorate the finished torte, as indicated above.

Lily Harmon's earliest memory is a recollection of a day spent in the attic of her New Haven childhood home, abandoned by her parents, who are absorbed with running their flourishing clothing business downtown. "The store is their natural habitat," she says in her recently published autobiography, *Freehand,* subtitled, "An Intimate Portrait of the New York Art Scene." Her mother is queen of the ladies' side of the family store, where "her greatest pleasure is outfitting brides." Meanwhile, Lily, who would marry five times in the course of her lifetime, is hidden upstairs in the cozy chamber, scribbling mermaids on the blank checks of her bankrupt uncle, embellishing "pay to the order of" with creatures with long wavy hair, tiny breasts, and fishtails for feet. Later, throughout her various residences, the attic, if it existed, would remain the place where she would choose to set up her studio.

Her youth was somewhat wild, she confesses. Invited not to return to Yale School of Art for failing the History of Ornament and for preferring to paint fresh fruit rather than dusty wax apples, she ships out to Paris. En route, she is given a string of pearls by a man who introduces himself as a prince. She is uncertain whether the necklace might have come from Tiffany's or Woolworth's, her benefactor eludes her attempt to return the necklace, and finally she gives it away spontaneously to a little girl she meets in a bistro, never knowing "if I have given away a czar's treasure or a five-and-ten-cent bauble." It is a lesson in the ambiguities of generosity that would haunt her career as an artist struggling to find ways to support herself. She modeled, worked as an art director in an advertising agency, picketed with WPA artists during the Depression, participated in founding Artist's Equity, and married the financier Joseph Hirshhorn, whose vast art collection would later find a home in the bagel-shaped Hirshhorn Museum and Sculpture Garden in Washington. All the while she painted, sustained by the philosophy her freehand life embodied, "to hold by letting go and to lose by holding." Her favorite books are writings by artists, such as Delacroix's *Journals* and Van Gogh's *Letters*. She is particularly noted for her portraits of friends and family, the image emerging from a skein of sketch lines, mottled like flesh on a skeleton. Often the same brushstrokes are shared by a neutral ground and the realized figure, so that the fight for emergence remains evident. The deep-set eyes, like wounds, are woefully sad, and the sitter sits with his inwardness compassionately exposed, with something of the defenselessness which the neglected Van Gogh expressed in his letters to his dear brother Theo, an art dealer who tried without success to sell the artist's paintings.

Lily Harmon has played an active part in the Provincetown art community for years, and many of its members have sat both for portraits and for her bountiful and festive meals, the result, she says, of an inherited inability to cook merely for two.

Sweet and Sour
Stuffed Cabbage

This will serve 4, but I usually make it for many more. It's ideal for a large party. Mimi Sheridan ate this at one of my parties, but when I gave her the recipe she was turned off by the Campbell's soup. So, it can also be made with canned Italian plum tomatoes, cooked down, or tomato sauce, or what you will.

1 large head of
  green cabbage
1½ lbs. ground chuck
1 large egg
2 handfuls corn flakes
1 handful uncooked rice
  (or parboil for 5 minutes
  and cool)
salt and pepper to taste
¾ to 1 cup of water
1 can Campbell's tomato
  soup (sometimes I add
  a little tomato paste)
1 soup can water
1 large onion, thinly sliced
½ lemon, thinly sliced
½ cup raisins
2 tablespoons sugar

Soak the cabbage in boiling water and separate the leaves. (This is the hard part. Do this little by little, putting the cabbage back into boiling water if necessary. You want the leaves loosened but not too soft. Of course, you will waste the core, since it won't do for wrapping.) Mix together in a bowl the ground meat, egg, corn flakes, rice, salt and pepper, and enough cold water to make the meat mixture light and fluffy. Form meat lightly into balls. Do not pack firmly; it tends to make the mixture heavy. Roll each ball into a cabbage leaf, folding the ends in. Place the little packages close together in a small roasting pan (I use a pretty yellow round paella pan in which to serve this). Pour the tomato soup, mixed with optional tomato paste and one can of water, over the meatballs. Cover with the thinly sliced onion and lemon, alternating them. It looks pretty and festive. Cover and bake in a slow oven—300°—for about 2½ to 3 hours, until brown. After one hour, sprinkle raisins and sugar over the cabbage leaves and continue baking.

The beauty part, as my grandmother used to say, is that there are no bones!

For a party, the less garbage the better—a good rule to follow. I find if I pack the little cabbages together, there is no need to tie them up in string as my grandmother used to do, because they will stay together nicely. Her way was like an obstacle course, picking bits of string out of your mouth.

Miriam Valente's Babka

2 squares of yeast, preferably fresh
⅔ cup milk, warmed
1½ cups sugar
½ lb. butter or margarine
3 eggs
3 cups flour, sifted
a pinch of salt
3 small cans candied fruit peel, such as pineapple, orange, lemon or citron, or cherry
raisins, cinnamon
nuts, chopped

Dissolve the yeast in the milk (warm but not too hot). Cream 3 tablespoons of the sugar into the butter or margarine. Separate the egg yolks from the whites, saving the whites. Add one yolk at a time to the creamed sugar and butter, and mix well. Add, alternately, the sifted flour and the milk-and-yeast mixture and season with a pinch of salt. Mix the dough thoroughly and store, covered, in the refrigerator until the next day.

The next day, beat the egg whites until they are stiff, to make meringue. Fold in the remaining sugar. Divide the dough into two parts. Roll out half the dough and spread with half the meringue. Sprinkle with candied fruits, raisins, nuts, and a little cinnamon. Roll up the babka, folding the edges to prevent leaking. Arrange the first roll in half of a well-greased pan (a babka pan with a hole in the middle is ideal). Do the same with the other half and join halves in the pan, forming a circle. Bake in a 375° oven for one hour. The babka may be started in a cool oven.

Barley Pilaf

To serve with pot roast, chicken, or other meat dishes, or with vegetables. Preheat oven to 350°.

1 large or 2 medium onions, chopped
½ lb. sliced mushrooms
¼ lb. butter or margarine
1½ cups pearl barley
1 quart chicken stock, fresh or canned
salt and pepper

Chop the onions coarsely and slice the mushrooms, thinly, through stem and all. Heat 2 tablespoons of butter or margarine in a large skillet and cook the mushrooms for about four minutes until the juices evaporate. Lift out and set aside. Add the remaining butter and cook the onions until they are wilted. Add the barley to the pan and cook gently until lightly browned. Add the mushrooms to the barley and onions. Pour on 1¾ cups of chicken stock. Bring to a boil, cover the pan tightly, and bake for 30 minutes. Remove cover. Taste for seasoning and add some salt and pepper at this point if you wish, then add another 1¾ cups of chicken stock. (The amount of liquid required may vary. You may need more or less liquid at this point; do not, however, let the pilaf get mushy.) Bake for another half an hour.

Renate Ponsold

Howie Schneider is most known for his comic strip *Eek and Meek,* syndicated nationwide in over 400 newspapers. He has drawn the two talking mice, Eek and Meek, for over 20 years, ever since he salvaged them from a run of cartoons, about government and science, that ran dry of ideas after two months. Schneider became exasperated by his characters, in particular a scientist who kept two mice as subjects for laboratory experiments. Impulsively, Schneider let the mice have their say. Eek, not yet named, materialized smoking a large cigar. When the other mouse asks, "Where'd you get that cigar?" Eek replies, "Oh, I'm smoking for the government. Cancer Research." So the other mouse says, "Big deal! I'm in genetics." From then on, Schneider says, "The two mice spoke to each other. All I had to do was take up a pen, and they'd start talking."

When Schneider sold *Eek and Meek* in 1965, after working in advertising and television in New York, he bought a house in Provincetown and moved here permanently. His small adjacent studio, flooded with light from the large windows opening on the bay, contains a drawing board and a swivelling, high-back leather chair surrounded by uniform volumes binding collections of his strips, piles of correspondence, and numerous works of sculpture, fashioned of clay or found wooden objects. These pieces, many of which have been exhibited in Provincetown galleries, are affectionate portraits of artist friends, such as Eddie Euler. Euler, a Provincetown artist who owned a dozen studios on Brewster Street, renting them to generations of artists, is memorialized in a clay bust that looks like the moral ghost of himself, his face existentially narrower than Giacometti's thin man, sitting like a tall rusted nail on his stool in the Beachcomber's, complaining unsteadily to no one in particular that the club was diluting its artist membership by admitting too many carpenters.

Schneider thinks Provincetown is a perfect place for a cartoonist to live. Where else can you stay at home and attend a scholarly James Joyce symposium in June and a transvestite convention in October, after all the tourists have gone? "A cartoonist," he says, "sees gaps and makes you aware of them. For instance, traditionally, Eek has never worked. His reason was that if he couldn't play the violin, he wasn't going to do anything, then finds he couldn't play the violin. When asked if he is still not working, he replies, '*I'm* unemployed...it's the economy that's not working.' "

Creamy Shrimp Salad

Terrific for cocktail parties. Serve with crackers or imported dark pumpernickel.

**1 lb. medium-size shrimp,
cooked and peeled**
1 pint sour cream
**1 12-oz. jar of
Hellman's mayonnaise**
**1 12-oz. jar of
Heinz chili sauce**
2 cups scallions, chopped

Mix together the sour cream, mayonnaise, and chili sauce. Mix in the shrimp and scallions.

This recipe is easily expanded: just use equal amounts of mayonnaise and chili sauce, and increase the amount of sour cream.

Real Swell Veal

2 veal chops
  (approximately 8 oz. each)
1 tablespoon corn oil
4 small potatoes, peeled
1 12-oz. can
  whole peeled tomatoes
3 oz. mozzarella cheese,
  thinly sliced
2 tablespoons Dijon mustard
2 tablespoons red wine
  vinegar
1 head of broccoli,
  cut into spears

Par-boil the potatoes. Braise the chops in a large cast-iron pan in corn oil until both sides are brown. Add the tomatoes to the pan and crush them onto the chops. Add the potatoes, placing them around the chops. Cook the chops in the pan for three more minutes. Lay the cheese slices across the chops and remove the pan from the flame. Place the pan in a preheated oven; bake at 350° for 30 minutes.

Serve the chops with the potatoes, and with broccoli, prepared as follows: Mix the mustard with the red wine vinegar. Steam the broccoli spears and splash the mustard-vinegar sauce over them in the serving dish. Serves two hungry people.

Chicken Isidor

This dish is light and easy to prepare. It's best served over rice pilaf.

1 chicken, cut up
1 12-oz. bottle
  Italian dressing
2 cups mushrooms, sliced
3 garlic cloves, minced
1 cup white wine
paprika
fresh rosemary

Place the cut-up chicken pieces in a pan, pour over them the Italian dressing (any brand will do), and marinate them for about two hours. Preheat oven to 350°. Add the sliced mushrooms and the minced garlic to the pan. Pour the wine evenly over the chicken pieces. Sprinkle the chicken with paprika and rosemary leaves. Bake for 50 minutes to an hour, basting every ten minutes.

MELISSA MEYER

Melissa Meyer began coming to Provincetown in the summers of the early seventies, studying at the painting workshop conducted by Leo Manso and Victor Candell. Manso was also her teacher in New York, and it was he who would recommend her for the Prix de Rome, a fellowship that enabled her to spend a year in Italy, where she learned about pasta and Piero della Francesca. Back in New York in her Tribeca loft, she hung large posters that amplified details of vaulting Renaissance spaces, a melancholy stillness hanging in the empty air, irradiated with colored dust. Meyer's own painting is based on the gestural practice of abstract expressionism, especially the wide-brushed calligraphic markings of de Kooning and Gorky, with the sudden shapes that emerge in the working process. "For my work to succeed," she says, "it should be concerned with reality, but that part of reality that is inexact, uncertain, mysterious, maybe anxious and in a state of becoming." Stylistically, she revitalizes these abstract expressionist values in the same way that Renaissance art refers to religious stories, saying "The story has already been told, but let me tell it again so you may understand."

Meyer shows regularly in New York at R.C. Erpf. She was also included in

Aimee Rentmeester

the 1988 exhibition at the Metropolitan Museum of Art, *A New Generation, the 80s, American Painters & Sculptors.* She tends to build up the surfaces of her work in oil and wax, sometimes scratching out an architecture in which space intermingles under shared arches. She has also done a number of drawings, exhibited recently in Provincetown at the J.L. Becker/East End Gallery.

Drawing and painting are related activities that feed on each other, she says. Some drawings she starts by marking the surface with white oil stick, leaving some of the white paper uncovered. Then black oil stick may be added to the surface of both whites. With other drawings, the lights are pulled out of the darks. She loves to cook, too, "but I like to eat more than I like to cook and I like to paint more than I like to cook," she says.

Pollo Arrosto
(Roast Chicken)

From Rosa's cookbook; Rosa lives in Valdottavo, eight miles north of Lucca, in Garfagnana, a particularly hilly area of western Tuscany, in Italy.

1 whole chicken
2 garlic cloves
7 fresh sage leaves
salt and pepper to taste
olive oil
½ cup red wine

Preheat the oven to 375°. Rinse the chicken in cold water and pat dry with paper towels. Mince the garlic and sage and combine with several tablespoons of olive oil and salt and pepper to taste. Place this mixture inside the cavity of the chicken, reserving some to rub over the outside. Place the chicken in a roasting pan in the oven at 375°. After about half an hour, pour the wine over the chicken and continue roasting. The chicken is usually done after about an hour, unless it is unusually large (allow 20 minutes per pound). When cooked, it should be golden brown, and the juice that runs from it when pricked with a fork should be clear.

Gelato Spazzacamino
(Chimneysweepers Ice Cream)

From Classic Italian Cooking, *by Marcella Hazan, this is an easy, Roman dessert.*

ice cream
espresso, uncooked,
powdered
scotch

Combine the ingredients to taste.

Pasta with Vodka

Taught to me by the artist Madeline Weinrib.

1 lb. fusilli pasta
3 cloves garlic, crushed
½ lb. bacon
4 oz. ham
1 carton heavy cream
1 carton half-and-half
crushed red pepper to taste
vodka
2 tablespoons olive oil
1 tablespoon butter
chopped parsley
grated Parmesan cheese

Cook the fusilli *al dente*.

Chop the bacon and ham and saute them in a pan. In another pan, saute the crushed garlic cloves in olive oil. Pour off the fat from the bacon and ham and add the meats to the garlic and olive oil. Add the butter. Pour in the half-and-half. Pour in the cream. Add salt to taste. Add some hot pepper and one or two shots of vodka. Cook this sauce over a medium flame.

Drain the pasta and pour it into a bowl. Pour on the sauce and stir it in. Garnish with parsley and Parmesan cheese. Serves 3–4.

"Ceres," etching on magnani paper

Ray Romanos Rizk learned about Middle-Eastern cooking from his mother, Latify Rizk, who came from the mountain village of Machghara in Lebanon. This village has a distinct reputation for its good cooking. The cooks of the nearby villages were consistently either good or bad, he says, since the society was very close knit and the same recipes were passed down from one generation to another, with little changes. In America, when Lebanese and Syrian immigrants gathered for church outings, the food brought by Machghara women was usually sought out first. It is these recipes that found their way to Provincetown when Rizk's mother would visit, preparing eastern meals for the crews of the restaurants of Ciro Cozzi and Sal Del Deo. In addition, when Helen and Napi Van Dereck opened their restaurant, they invited Latify to demonstrate in their kitchen, influencing the menu to this day.

Risk began his career as a landscape and portrait painter in New York City, after having studied with Henry Hensche in 1949 and 1950. But then, with his wife, Grace, returning to Provincetown permanently in 1952, he established his studio there. Playing music on the Greek bouzouki, a long-necked stringed instrument resembling a large mandolin, he learned the value of improvisation in traditional Middle-Eastern music, where the themes or modes are the basis for melodic variations. In 1958, struggling to open a stubborn door to his studio on a particularly windy day, a can of stain flew from his hand and splashed a design on a bare white canvas, a "magnificent accident," he says, teaching him how he might use paint improvisationally. Since then, he has painted in an abstract expressionistic style. Each work is titled "One with the Tao," and given a sequential number.

He shows in various galleries around the country and his work is in over 40 corporate collections, including the Bell Telephone Headquarters in Detroit, where six paintings hang in the "Rizk Conference Room." A Detroit talk-show host described him as the "Rembrandt of corporate art," an amusing appellation for a painter who likens the process of painting to doing battle like a Samurai swordsman, approaching the canvas in a spontaneous manner without entertaining thoughts of success or failure. "Developing the art," he says, "meant developing the man, relating creative action to action in life — a spontaneous action that is a result of awareness and clarity."

Hummus B'Tahini

1 15-oz. can chickpeas
½ scant cup tahini
juice and pulp of 1½ large or
  2 small lemons
1 teaspoon salt
½ to ¾ teaspoon
  garlic powder

In a blender, mix the lemon juice, salt, garlic, and tahini. Then gradually add the chickpeas, 1 to 2 tablespoons at a time, with just a little liquid from the can, blending after each addition. When complete, the consistency should be that of sour cream.

As a dip, hummus can be served plain or with a small amount of olive oil poured on top in the center. Garnish with paprika and sprigs of fresh parsley. Middle Easterners enjoy eating it with pieces of Syrian bread and raw onion.

Baba Ghannouj

A variation of Hummus B'Tahini is Baba Ghannouj using eggplant instead of chickpeas. The resulting dish has an unusually interesting smoky flavor, because the eggplant is cooked in its skin by placing it over or under an open flame.

1 medium eggplant
½ scant cup tahini
juice and pulp of 1½ large or
  2 small lemons
1 teaspoon salt
½ to ¾ teaspoon
  garlic powder

Char the eggplant by placing it over or under an open flame, using either charcoal or an oven broiler. Turn the eggplant occasionally to cook on all sides, until it is cooked through. The burned skin, which gives it the smoky flavor and aroma, should then be removed. Mash the eggplant together with the other ingredients, and serve in the same manner as Hummus B'Tahini.

Lamb and Rice Pilaf

2 cups long grain white rice
1 lb. lean lamb, chopped,
   diced, or coarsely ground
¼ cup olive oil
3 medium onions, chopped
3 oz. pine nuts or
   slivered almonds
2 cups beef stock or broth
2 cups water
2 tablespoon butter
½ teaspoon allspice
¼ teaspoon cinnamon
salt and pepper to taste

Saute the onions in olive oil until translucent, and set aside. In a large pan, saute the nuts in butter until light brown, stirring constantly. Add the rice to the pan and mix well to coat the grains with butter. Then immediately add the stock, water, lamb, onions, spices and seasonings. Cover with a tight lid and bring to a boil. Then reduce the heat to medium and cook, for approximately 30 minutes, or until the rice is cooked and the lamb is tender.

Baked Eggplant with Lamb

3 medium eggplants
1½ lbs. lean lamb, cut into
   ½-inch cubes or
   coarsely ground (beef may
   be used instead)
3 medium onions, chopped
3 cans tomato sauce
2 oz. pine nuts (optional)
3 garlic cloves, mashed, or
   1 teaspoon garlic powder
¼ teaspoon allspice
1/8 teaspoon cinnamon
1 teaspoon dried mint
salt and pepper to taste
olive oil

In a bowl, mix the meat, garlic, onions, spices, mint and nuts. Peel the eggplants and slice them into ¼-inch rounds. Coat the bottom of a deep baking pan (approximately 12'' × 16'') with a thin film of olive oil.

Layer the ingredients in the pan, starting with the tomato sauce. Then add a single layer of eggplant slices, and some of the meat mixture. Repeat until the ingredients are used up, ending with tomato sauce. (Sprinkle some grated cheese on top, if you wish.) Cover the pan with tin foil and bake at 350° for approximately one hour, or until the eggplant is cooked. Serve with Syrian Rice.

Syrian Rice

2 cups long grain white rice
3 oz. pine nuts
   or slivered almonds
½ cup orzo (rice-shaped
   macaroni) or thin spaghetti
   broken into 1-inch lengths
2 tablespoons butter
4 cups water
salt to taste

Saute the nuts in butter until they turn a very pale tan. Add the pasta. Stir constantly until both are light brown. Add the rice and mix briefly to coat with the butter mixture. Add the water and salt. Cook until the rice is done and all of the water has been absorbed.

Stuffed Grape Leaves

Pick grape leaves from your own vines, or from those of anyone else who will give you permission; it does not hurt the vine. On Cape Cod, vines grow wild in many wooded areas; these leaves can also be used. The best time to pick the leaves is usually in the early summer, before August, while the leaves are still tender. If you pick them later in the season, choose only the tender leaves that are not matte, but shiny on one side, regardless of the size of the leaves. Large leaves can be just as tender as small ones.

Basic Stuffing

Combine in a bowl and mix:
½ lb. lean lamb or beef,
coarsely ground
1 cup long grain white rice
¼ teaspoon allspice
⅛ teaspoon cinnamon
2 cloves garlic, mashed, or
½ teaspoon garlic powder
salt and pepper to taste

1 12-oz. can tomato juice
40 to 50 grape leaves

Rinse leaves well in cold water, then place the leaves in a pot of boiling water for 2 to 3 minutes to soften them slightly. Remove them from the water and place them on a large board or tray to cool. Place a spoonful of stuffing in the center of each leaf and roll into a cigar shape, folding in the ends. Do not over-pack the leaves, as the rice will expand when cooked. Carefully stack the stuffed leaves in a large pot and add the tomato juice and enough water to cover the rolls. Cook over medium heat for 30 minutes or until the rice is cooked.

This basic stuffing mix may also be used to stuff various vegetables:

Stuffed Summer Vegetables

24 small or 18 medium
yellow summer squash, or
24 small or
18 medium zucchini, or
6 or 8 bell peppers,
depending on size
Basic Stuffing (see under
Stuffed Grape Leaves)
1 12 oz. can tomato juice

Cut off the stem end, then scoop out the center of each zucchini with a teaspoon or a special tool purchased at a Middle Eastern grocery store, leaving a ¼- to ½-inch wall all around and on the bottom. (Save the scoopings to use in another recipe.*) Fill the vegetables with the stuffing—do not pack tightly, as rice expands when cooked. Stack them in a pot. Add one 12-oz. can of tomato juice, or a large can of tomatoes, chopped up, and enough water to cover the squash. Cook over medium heat 30 minutes or until the rice is cooked.

For stuffing bell peppers: Cut off the stem end and remove the seeds and membranes. Fill with the stuffing and cook as squash.

Basic Stuffing Variations: You can add numerous ingredients, as desired, to the basic stuffing, such as chopped onions (either raw or sauteed), pine nuts, or raisins. Chickpeas (soaked overnight) can be used in place of meat, or you can use ground sausage (such as linguica). Also, bulgar wheat can be used in place of rice.

This recipe is also excellent for stuffing cabbage leaves; use one medium-sized head of cabbage.

*A note on the squash scoopings: to make Eggs and Squash, mix the scooped-out insides of zucchini or summer squash with sauteed onions, eggs, and salt. Either scramble together or cook as an omelette.

Sim-Sum Squares

This is a holiday candy recipe Grace Rizk learned from her Russian-Jewish grandmother. It was a favorite with the children in the family.

½ cup honey
  (natural uncooked)
½ cup sugar
¼ cup hot water
pinch of salt
1 cup sesame seeds
  (sim-sum)
½ cup chopped walnuts,
  almonds, or pistachios

In the top of a double-boiler, combine the honey, sugar, and hot water. Bring to a boil, add salt, and lower the flame to moderate heat. Stir constantly to prevent burning. Cook to the soft-ball stage. Add sesame seeds and nuts, and cook over hot water for three minutes, constantly stirring. Now take the top part of the double-boiler off the bottom part, put it directly on moderate heat, and keep stirring for about five minutes, or until the candy is golden brown. Pour the mixture onto a wet board and pat it down to a ½-inch thickness. Dip a knife blade in hot water and cut the candy into small squares or diamonds. The mixture hardens quickly, so work fast.

A favorite, formative book for Joyce Johnson was Defoe's *Robinson Crusoe,* in which the hero, shipwrecked on what he thought was a deserted island, is obliged to survive using his ingenuity and the few tools that have not sunk with his ship. Crusoe says in his account, "I was at a great loss about my tools. I had three large axes, and an abundance of hatchets (for we carried the hatchets for traffic with the Indians), but with much chopping and cutting knotty hard wood, they were all full of notches and dull; and though I had a grindstone, I could not turn it and grind my tools too. This cost me as much thought as a statesman would have bestowed upon a grand point of politics, or a judge upon the life and death of a man." While she was creating, Crusoe-like, from scratch, Truro's Castle Hill Center for the Arts (which she started with a $350 loan on her credit card, recruiting faculty, developing the curriculum, writing grants, drumming up publicity, and raising funds), she also, simultaneously, built her own house nearby. One of the rooms was entirely fabricated from castaways at the dump, except for the two-by-fours and nails. When a mason did not appear as promised, she mixed the cement, laid the footings, and buttered and set the bricks herself. She lives without electricity, except for the occasion when she rigs her TV set to the battery of her Toyota pickup, and her kitchen functions on bottled gas. "As an artist-teacher," she said, "my income is necessarily limited. In order to have time to sculpt, I can only be employed part of the time, which means living frugally and not getting trapped by heavy mortgages." She has made a virtue of necessity, admitting, "there are mistakes in the construction of the house and studios, but that makes them more human, part of me and my frailties."

She has worked as an arts reporter for the Provincetown *Advocate, The Cape Codder,* and *CapeArts* magazine. She produces a biweekly oral history program for WOMR radio, teaches sculpture during the winter at the Art Association, and takes striking photographs of aspects of the landscape that are seldom seen, such as the dunes after a snowstorm. In her sculpture, her esthetic develops from an appreciation of the organic nature of plant life, how things grow out of themselves. Working with clay, wood, and stone, she shapes totemic, off-balance, undulating images, with stems splitting and pods stacked one upon the other. Her varied, pioneering activities in encouraging local artists and culture are consistent with her own work as an artist and are based on an understanding of solitary effort. She realizes, "It is brutal to survive on the Provincetown economy, and until you understand that, it is hard to understand the artists here. Many are primitives. Primitives have style without knowledge. The town is not media-dominated. You are thrown upon your own resources, and you have the opportunity to develop a continuity with yourself without distractions."

Cranberry Sauce

The trick to making fresh cranberry sauce that has a wonderful zest to it is not to overcook the berries. The whole process should not take more than five minutes.

4 cups fresh whole cranberries
¾ cup sugar
¼ cup water

Put the ingredients in a heavy cooking pan. Place over medium high heat (if using an electric stove, heat the coils before placing the pan on them). Stir and turn over the berries continuously until water and juice begin to boil. When the entire mix looks as though it is beginning to boil, remove it from the heat and put a lid on the pan. Let cool.

I repeat: the entire process should not take more than five minutes. The results should be whole, glazed cranberries in sauce.

"Woman in Hat," study for bronze figure

Quince Paste
(also called Membrillo)

The quince is a fruit tree that grows in New England. It has flat, pear-shaped fruit that is deep yellow and sweetly pungent when fully ripe. Quince paste is a thick loaf sweet that can be sliced. It is commonly found in Spanish-speaking countries, but seldom here, perhaps because it is very messy to make. But the rewards are worth it. A slice of membrillo with a slice of sharp cheese is a memorable dessert or snack.

whole ripe quinces
equal amount of sugar
water

To make quince paste, put the whole fruit in a two- to four-quart pot with enough water almost to cover. Simmer until the fruit is soft but still firm. Cool. Remove the cores of the quinces. Put the remaining skin and flesh through a food grinder or *pureer*. Combine one part quince puree with one part sugar. Simmer over low heat, stirring frequently so that the mixture does not *catch*. Be careful when stirring that the mixture does not splatter on face or hands, because it will stick and burn. If you have a candy thermometer, cook to the soft-ball point. Otherwise, cook until it is very thick and a deep rose color. Wet the bottoms of loaf pans or cake pans with cold water, and dump excess out without drying bottom of pans. Pour in the quince mixture. Let set overnight.

I have never been able to understand why sometimes the mixture sets up overnight and other times it takes several days and turnings. If slices cannot be cut easily, then the mixture should be turned into another pan, wet as before, so that the bottom part is now on top and has a chance to air. You may have to spoon some of the mixture into the second pan. Transfer the mixture from one pan to another with a day or so of setting, until it is firm enough to slice.

To store, cut into 2 x 4 inch squares and wrap in waxed paper. Place in a cool spot, where it will keep indefinitely. Sometimes a little mold forms on the surface; just scrape it off.

Nancy Webb had studied painting and printmaking, served as the art director of the Noonday Press in New York, and was the author/illustrator of several books, before beginning to make sculpture in 1965. Bringing up three children, she developed an increased attraction to the sculpture she saw at exhibitions, finding herself drawn to it in preference to paintings, perhaps, she says, because she was a mother who had babies and "wanted to experience things." She took an extended apprenticeship at the Tallix Foundry in Beacon, New York. She had been working only a few years when she made a statement about her sculpture which she says remains essentially true today: "My work is derived from natural forms, animal (including the human), insect, fish (including the crustaceans), and vegetable. In the process of transforming these creatures in bronze (for me, a marvelously living material), they are modified, changed, as though to present an additional order of life. Quite often I use dead forms, skulls, skeletons, dried flowers or bodies of insects. But my interest is not simply in the fact that they are dead, left-over, but also in the mysterious power that is retained within these intricate structures. A friend once said of my work that it was 'a dream of nature.' I would agree as long as among the dreams would be included the nightmare."

There is a dark side to her imagination which is fascinated by fossilized organic shapes, like the moon snail, bulbous, bony, often broken, revealing a

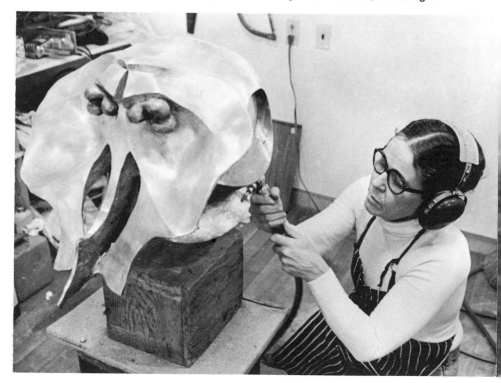

spiraling inner core through the fracture, dense and thick with concentric concentrations of its own growth. Something about the knowledge that her shapes were once organic makes their bronze permanence forbidding. In the transformation, the contours are smoothed, edges are adjusted to echo other edges, and a process of essentialization is completed. Nature is taken out of nature. One is reminded that "death" is a metaphor in mythology, expressing a radical shift in consciousness, the "afterlife" being imagined by the living as a psychological realm with an eternal present, necessarily haunted by the ghost of a transitory present. Reproduced in this book is Nancy Webb's "Agamemnon," originally modeled in wax, and based on a dolphin skull her son found washed up on a Carolina ocean beach. She wished to give it another form of life. The helmeted shape reminded her of a death mask of Agamemnon, the war-driven Greek who sacrificed his own daughter in preparation for his siege of Troy. In its inhuman symmetry, inspiring both pity and fear, the piece suggests the demonic Darth Vader, perhaps Agamemnon's modern incarnation. Although her most recent series of sculptures focuses on fertility figures, she says that they are also "a little frightening, the way life is."

Nancy Webb is the mother of three talented artists in their own right: Alex, a documentary photographer; Sophie, an ornithologist specializing in drawing birds; and Patrick, a painter who shows in New York, Boston and the Outer Cape. She is married to Dwight Webb, a former publisher who serves very actively as an instrument of intelligence on the Fine Arts Work Center Writing Committee. With references to his readings in mythology and Jung, he describes Nancy as "doing archetypes."

"Agamemnon," bronze

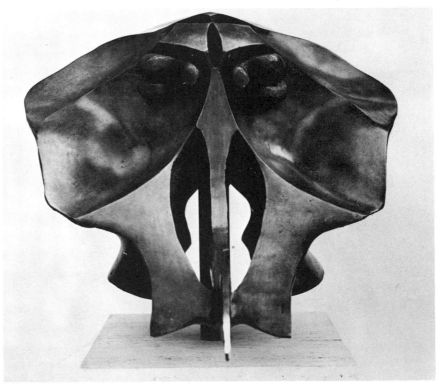

Edible Cauliflower

1 head cauliflower, cut
  into flowerettes
½ nutmeg, grated
pepper to taste
1 small onion, sliced
¾ cup low-fat cottage cheese
1 egg
paprika

Cook the cauliflower in 2 quarts of boiling water for 5 minutes; drain the cauliflower and put it in the bowl of a food processor with the onion, nutmeg, pepper, cottage cheese, and egg. Process for 2 minutes, then put the mixture in a baking dish, dust the top with paprika, and bake the casserole in a 350° oven for 30 minutes.

Gnocchi Nancy Webb

1 1-lb. package
  potato gnocchi*
2 large onions, chopped
8 oz. mushrooms, sliced**
2 veal sausages (bratwurst),
  sliced in ½-inch slices
4 tablespoons garlic-flavored
  olive oil
1 cup low-fat cottage cheese
3 oz. hard ricotta cheese
½ cup fresh parsley, chopped
3 large garlic cloves, minced
1 egg
1 heaping tablespoon
  fresh oregano†, chopped
1 heaping tablespoon
  fresh rosemary, chopped
Pamesan cheese, to taste

Cook the gnocchi in 3 quarts of boiling water for ten minutes. Drain and let stand. Saute the onions in a pan with 2 tablespoons of oil until golden brown. Saute the mushrooms and sausage in another pan with 2 tablespoons of oil. Put into a food processor the parsley, garlic cloves, cottage cheese, ricotta, and egg; process for one minute using the chopped blade. Add this mixture to the onions, mushrooms, and sausage; mix in the chopped rosemary and oregano. Take a pan (8½" × 3" or the equivalent size), pour half of the sauce on the bottom; add gnocchi, then the rest of the sauce, and mix. Sprinkle with Parmesan cheese, cover, and bake at 350° for 20 minutes; uncover and finish cooking another 10 minutes. Serves 4

*Frozen potato gnocchi are available on the Cape at the Stop & Shop in Orleans.

**The best mushrooms for this are large Italian fungi—3 will do; next best, Italian brown crimini. However, this recipe works quite well with ordinary domestic mushrooms.

†If you cannot use or find fresh oregano or rosemary, I suggest one teaspoon of dried oregano and ½ teaspoon of dried thyme (dried rosemary tends to resemble Cape Cod pine needles). Fresh basil is great in this dish. There are indeed numerous substitutions one can make.

Nut Cake

For this cake you must have a food processor and a 9"× 3" spring-form pan. It can be done by hand, but I hate to think of the man-hours involved. Without a spring-form pan you may well end up with pieces of cake.

1 cup dark brown sugar, loosely packed
3½ cups filberts
9 eggs
2 tablespoons almond extract
confectioners' sugar

Put the nuts in a food processor with the chopping blade, and make them into nut flour. Do not process them too long or you will have nut butter. Nut flour has a rather coarse consistency, like that of oatmeal. Do not try for finer things! Remove the nut flour and put it in a large bowl. Separate 8 eggs; put the yolks in the food processor and the whites in another large bowl. Add the brown sugar, one whole egg, and the almond extract to the egg yolks in the food processor. Process for one minute, then add this mixture to the nut flour in the bowl; stir it well.

Beat the whites of eggs in the other large bowl until they have stiff peaks; then fold in the nut mixture from the other bowl. (Be sure to cut and fold.)

Grease and lightly flour the spring-form pan; pour in the cake mixture and put it in a pre-heated oven at 325° for one hour and fifteen minutes. (If you need to test it, take a straw and put it in the middle of the cake. If the straw comes out clean, your cake is done—otherwise, wait! wait!)

Take the cake out of the oven, let it cool, and remove it from the pan by running a knife around the edges. Then, when the side of the pan is removed, run a knife under the bottom. Slide the cake onto a plate and dust it lightly with confectioners' sugar.

This is a very rich cake. At a party it should feed 12 not-too-greedy people. It freezes very well. This cake can be made with other nuts—pecans or walnuts. If you use walnuts, put in a bit more sugar—walnuts are slightly bitter. Almonds are too oily. I do prefer filberts for this cake.

Richard Smith is a quiet, persistent artist respected by many fellow artists. He is an artist's artist, following the leads in his own work, rather than the lures of the bitch goddess. Arriving in Provincetown from West Virginia, he lived alone for a decade, making paintings and box constructions. Behind glass, he displayed peaks into an imaginary attic, where old maps, toy skulls, the rubber heads of chubby dolls, and other small objects found cunningly at yard sales, were reduced to the coherence of a total world, in the manner of Joseph Cornell. Meanwhile, in Poland, Ewa Nogiec was at the State College of Art in Poznan, when, with two months remaining for the completion of her master's degree, she left for the United States. She intended to return shortly, since Solidarity was at that time very strong, but soon there was a fear that the Russians would suppress freedom as they had done in Czechoslovakia and Hungary. Thinking "how history changes, how fast," she

lived with an aunt in New York. The big city was "pure city, too strange, too big." She had never seen black people. In her painting, black became the color of the unknown, and she wrote her father, "My black is somehow like a coat through which my figures and forms are ploughing. It is a skin with an underlife, not a background. Even in collage, where I paste faces and figures on black, they emerge through the black to show their fears and obsessions. This is my language."

She heard there was an art colony in Provincetown, from a Polish friend who had lived in Wellfleet. She came, and after spending the summer selling candy, she decided to live here, supporting herself by doing layout and design at the *Advocate* and at *Provincetown Magazine.* She exhibits her paintings and collages at the David Brown Gallery. After she and Richard married, he took up windsurfing, spending afternoons criss-crossing the bay, and finding back in his studio that his painting had changed. He recalls, "In frustration at not being able to make a painting work, I cut it up into strips and wove them randomly. The result was so surprising to me that I began cutting and weaving all sorts of two-dimensional images. The most satisfying were done with small black-and-white targets normally used in rifle practice." His recent drawings, such as the one illustrated here, though it only implies weaving, was done from those small weavings.

Hot Mead (Krupnik)

Krupnik is one of the oldest-known drinks in Poland, dating far back into the Middle Ages. References to it are found in literature, folk songs, and poetry. Drunk in large quantities, it was supposed to fell strong warriors and conquer conquerors.

1 cup honey
1 cup water
3 or 4 cloves
6 sticks cinnamon
a small piece of nutmeg, or
¼ teaspoon ground nutmeg
1 3-inch piece vanilla bean
a ½-inch strip orange rind
2 cups pure alcohol

Bring honey and water to a boil and carefully remove all scum. Add cloves, cinnamon, nutmeg, vanilla bean, and orange rind. Allow to boil up again, remove from heat, let stand for a minute or two, and again bring to a boil. Cover and set aside for at least half an hour to steep. Strain, again bring to a boil, and then pour in the alcohol. Stir well and serve piping hot.

Ewa Nogiec, "Untitled"

Salsa Cruda

This raw vegetable table sauce accompanies many Mexican foods. The fresh cilantro gives it a unique flavor.

3 or 4 tomatoes
1 bunch fresh cilantro
1 onion
1 garlic clove
1 or more jalapeno or
serrano chilies
1 tablespoon vinegar
salt

Finely chop all ingredients and combine with the salt and vinegar in a bowl. Salsa can also be served as an appetizer, accompanied by tortilla chips and Corona beer.

Richard Smith, pen and ink drawing

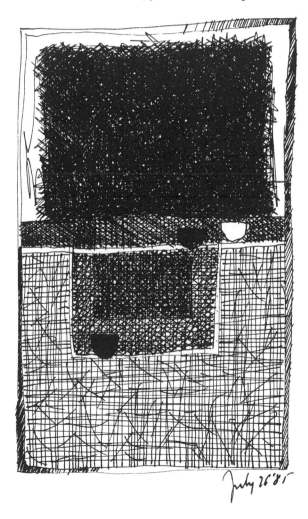

As an artist, Peter Hutchinson has taken upon himself the meta-task of redefining the context of art, such that his productions always require a verbal frame, which he sort of supplies, the way an ant's back bows parabolically against the burden of weight greater than itself. His work symbolically combines words and pictures, either in the classically emblematic manner of "Painting and Eating," reproduced in this book, where title, picture and text combine to make a total statement about the interaction of art and life, or in the apparently arbitrary way a common adventure is able to generate a poetic narrative, as in "Foraging: Being an Account of a Hike through the Snowmass Wilderness as a Work of Art." In "Foraging," published in *Art in America* in 1972, Hutchinson describes his six-day backpack hike with a companion, in which they took photographs, made a movie, "foraged" for some shepherd's-purse in flower, some violets, a few leaves of alpine lily, mushrooms and wild strawberries.

One morning, after sleeping through a thunderstorm and waking fitfully for brief seconds to a brumous moon-tinted night, he has "the sense of being utterly diffuse, of being everywhere, of having no possessions but possessing everything." Between getting sick on the wrong mushrooms and getting up in the middle of the night "to photograph by moonlight a ghostly drift of seeding dandelions, each a small moon," there is an odd urgency about Hutchinson's observation, "I tell Jonathan that I must do some foraging today or the title of the piece will sound nonsensical." The piece ends after six days when Hutchinson writes "The End" in wild strawberries, which, when photographed, cast shadows of the early morning sun, giving the letters "a sort of scripted depth." With the suggestion that life becomes art on the occasion where art becomes organic, like life, imprisoned in a natural cycle, Hutchinson's companion eats the wild strawberries, and completes the work of art by destroying "The End."

Peter Hutchinson was born in England, but educated in the United States at the University of Illinois, where he nourished himself by eating many beefsteak mushrooms and where he majored in plant genetics before switching to art. A pioneer of art that deals with ecology and the earth, with stories created by enacting a dream project in real time, Hutchinson has work in the collection of the Museum of Modern Art and shows regularly in New

York at the John Gibson Gallery, whose stable has included Vito Acconci and Dennis Oppenheim. Since 1976, he has lived yearround in Provincetown, working in a small studio behind his little, ship-tidy house. Nearby he cultivates an elaborate quarter-acre garden which microcosmically recreates the whole world, where, for example, the alps rise in his rock garden, the Sahara sits in his sand dune and "Japan" is the irregular table with the pots of bonzai.

November, 1973

Painting and Eating

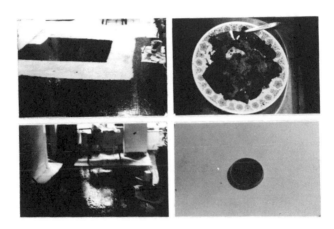

I was painting the floor and then stopped to make lunch. While I was sprinkling sesame seeds on the vegetables, some fell onto the wet top of the paint can. This created an object wherein the two activities of painting and eating came together.

Peter Hutchinson

Wild Mushroom Salad

Boletus edulis **and other**
   edible *boletes*
Agaricus campestris
string beans
bean sprouts
grated carrots
kidney beans, cooked
olive oil
vinegar
garlic
tamari

Marinate the kidney beans in olive oil, vinegar, garlic, and a little tamari for several hours. Clean and chop the other ingredients and combine them with the marinated beans in a large dish. Chill and serve.

Wild Mushrooms Baked with Carrots

4 or 5 *Boletes edulis*
½ lb. carrots,
   scraped and sliced
1 handful sunflower seeds
2 tablespoons sesame seeds
¼ cup olive oil
sea salt, to taste

Carefully brush the *boletes* free of sand and dirt, and slice them lengthwise (down the stalk) into several pieces. Parboil the carrots. Place the mushrooms and carrots in a baking tray. Sprinkle with the seeds and sea salt. Pour the olive oil evenly over the vegetables. Bake at 350° until slightly browned.

Fruit Yogurt

2 cups dried milk
4 cups water
3 tablespoons live yogurt
   culture
bananas
homemade blueberry jam
   in honey

To make the yogurt: combine the dried milk and the water. Bring to a boil, cool to luke warm, and add the yogurt culture. Keep at around 75° to 80° for 10 to 15 hours. Refrigerate the yogurt.
   Serve with sliced ripe bananas and homemade jam.

Dinner of Champignons

Hors d'Oeuvres
Pickled cèpes & gherkins

Soup
Russulas and agaricus campestris
in bean stock

Entrée
Baked Boletus edulis with carrots and sunflower
and sesame seeds
        with
Lactarius laccata, B. edulis & Agaricus campestris,
green pepper and onion tempura

Salad
Cèpes and A. campestris, cucumber, raw string
beans, bean sprouts and grated carrots & beans
in vinegar, olive oil and garlic.

Dessert
Fruit yogurt — bananas and yogurt flavored
with home-made blueberry jam in honey.

Home-made bread
Red zinger tea
Coffee
Carrot juice

In the course of a painting career that began in 1945, with a New York exhibition at the artist's cooperative called the Jane Street Gallery, Judith Rothschild has developed an art of incorporating two or three central ideas which are apparently in opposition to each other. Her paintings present, as if on a stage, a dialogue between clarity and chaos, between incisively shaped humanoid or plantlike forms and abstract rectangles of darkness, which she has lately been calling "black holes." A persistent classicist, she often includes landscape motifs (visibly influenced by her long colloquy with Cape scenes) that are decidedly romantic in tenor. These are placed within a severely organized spatial structure, over which float relief elements shaped like isolated body parts ("many suggest broken shards and other debris of civilization," she says). These raised forms are sliced out of Foamcore and coated with plastic, or, more recently, they are sheets of extruded aluminum shaped and painted. Somewhere on the canvas there will be a heavily-brushed passage of action painting, sharply defined like a window in a wall, so that it is as if one looks through the surface of the painting out toward a vista called "painting as nature."

Rothschild first came to Provincetown in 1947, renting a small stable-loft in the west end that had previously been used by Jackson Pollock and later was the start of what became Franz Kline's studio. Having studied with Hans Hofmann in New York, she gradually came to know the Hofmanns as friends. Hofmann she remembers as "warm, open, and never pretentious." They became neighbors when she and her new husband, Anton Myer, a writer, bought a net-mending shack on the water across from the Hofmann's house. On one visit, immediately after toasting the newlyweds, Miz Hofmann celebrated the occasion by teaching Rothschild how to make potato dumplings, without which, it was suggested, no marriage between two artists could survive.

Rothschild was an active participant in the excitement of Forum '49, the series of exhibitions, programs and lectures held in Provincetown during the summer of 1949. "Due to the dynamism and idealism of Weldon Kees, its founder, Forum '49 became the articulate focus of the creative energy of that time," she says. She developed a deep friendship with Ann and Weldon Kees, resulting in a move the following spring to Northern California. For the next 14 years she lived in Big Sur and Monterey, returning to the Cape when possible, and exhibiting occasionally at the HCE Gallery in Provincetown. In the early 60s she bought an old farmhouse on Bound Brook Island in Wellfleet. Since then, every summer, she has worked in a studio she added. In 1977 she became a founding member of Provincetown's Long Point Gallery, a distinguished artist's cooperative embodying many of the values of Forum '49.

A recent series of paintings are titled "The Shield of Achilles." Most of them are linked metaphorically to her reading of Homer, and she wrote in a journal: "I keep being drawn back to memories of *The Illiad*. But really beneath is a simple fascination: the dichotomies, the violent emblematic contrasts in life between pleasure and war. Briseis is a slave for Achilles' pleasure, and I envision them before they are separated enjoying themselves on an Aegean beach. They are made all the more alluring by the impending threat of disaster. Can I get these two opposing feelings condensed into a single small rectangle, a rectangle that is, finally, unified?" In a male poem about male heroism, perhaps she has found an allegory for a feminine perspective on the iconoclastic condition of being a modern artist.

"Achilles and Briseis XXX"

Rolled Breast of Chicken with Sun-dried Tomatoes

I wanted to contribute a recipe that I think is really fun, and, as far as I know, original, and this one also meets my other key criteria: all ingredients are readily available and not extravagantly expensive; most of the dish can be prepared ahead of time, and there is nothing about it that makes it difficult to finish at the last minute if guests are late or the hour is extended; it's quick to prepare; and its originality is not so extreme as to be hazardous!

2 large chicken breasts,
  boned
1 jar sun-dried tomatoes in oil
3 artichoke bottoms, cooked
  in seasoned broth
  (or artichoke paste)
4 tablespoons creme fraiche
2 teaspoons Parmesan cheese
1 lb. spinach, chopped
  and steamed, or
½ lb. prosciutto

Take the boned chicken breasts and lay them out on a countertop. In a straight line across their length, place a small quantity of sun-dried tomatoes and an even smaller amount of prosciutto, making a red line running the length of the chicken. Now roll the chicken tightly, making a solid cylinder with a diameter of about 1¾ to 2 inches. Tuck in the ends neatly. Place the roll on a large piece of foil and wrap it very tightly, twisting the ends so that the entire object looks like a magnified "snapper," such as children have at parties. Make sure that there are several layers of foil so that no liquid can penetrate inside the wrapping. Each "snapper" should be about 12 to 15 inches long. Two such rolls should be sufficient for six people. Place the chicken rolls in a pan large enough to hold them comfortably. On the top of the stove, simmer the chicken rolls in water for about 30 minutes, adding hot water in the process so that the chicken is really being steamed rather than boiled.

Sauce: Take three artichoke bottoms that have been cooked in a well-seasoned broth (perhaps with some garlic) and mash them to a fairly coarse paste. (Jars of artichoke paste are now available, but they are relatively bland, so you should increase the quantity of artichoke to balance the flavor.) Add about six large pieces of sun-dried tomatoes, including some of the oil. Stir this mixture into four heaping tablespoons of *creme fraiche* or *quarte*, softened and heated in a pan, and about two generous teaspoons of the best grated Parmesan you can get (preferably Reggiano). When these ingredients are hot, test to correct seasoning, adding more tomato or cheese to taste. Yogurt can, if absolutely necessary, be substituted for the creme fraiche, or to dilute it.

Unwrap the "snappers" and arrange them on a bed of either prosciutto or fresh, lightly cooked spinach. Cut the chicken into slices about ⅜-inch thick and cover them with sauce. This dish may be served at room temperature. Serves 6.

Robert Motherwell spent his first summer in Provincetown in 1942, when he was 27 and had been painting seriously for one year. A graduate of Stanford University with a BA in philosophy, he had attended Harvard as a graduate student in esthetics, gone to Paris to research a thesis on Delacroix's *Journals*, then enrolled at Columbia University in New York to study art history under Meyer Schapiro. The celebrated art historian suggested that Motherwell devote himself to painting, rather than scholarship, after Motherwell knocked at his door once too often at eleven o'clock at night with his latest painting under his arm. Very quickly, Motherwell began to meet his contemporaries, as well as the Parisian artists who were exiled in New York during the war. He recalls, "I had a firm intuition as a stranger that the New York painting scene was filled with technical talent, but lacked an original creative principle, so that its work appeared one

RENATE PONSOLD

"MOSTLY ARTISTS"
PHOTOGRAPHS 1958-1977

step removed in origin." From the French surrealists he adapted their method of preconscious doodling called psychic automatism The advantage of the doodle, Motherwell found, was that it was one's own. As a method, rather than a style, the doodle is not a copying of anything, but an endlessly fertile way of revealing one's being to oneself. He observes, "If one works in an office where there is a telephone pad kept nearby for a long time, people will tend to doodle on that pad. After a while you can tell who used the phone last." The absent-minded aspect usually attribute to the doodle betrays the serious opportunity it offers to bring out in any given individual what he likes as he develops it. Motherwell's audacious achievement perhaps lies in his insistence on the intuitional basis of what others perceive as an intellectual process, for the painting, he says, "comes out of the correction of mistakes through feeling."

After spending summers in East Hampton, Motherwell returned to Provincetown briefly in 1949 to give a lecture for "Forum '49" at the Art Association. He remembers "being struck by the simplicity and physical closeness of Provincetown compared to the status-consciousness and spread-outness of East Hampton." By the mid-fifties, he was returning regularly, enjoying concentrated painting periods where he was able to produce half a year's work in three months. Living in the East End, "within a stone's throw of Allerton Street, ideal for children," he first had a studio at the Eulers' on Brewster Street, then in the large barn at Days Lumberyard (now the Fine Arts Work Center), incorporating the arched doors of the barn into the Spanish balconies on the street side of his present studio-house at 631 Commercial Street. Motherwell, who admits to being shy and diffident socially ("although not in my studio''), finds an equivalent for street life as he lunches under his cafe umbrella on the bayside of his house, where, at low tide, the sand flats are peopled by *flaneurs*.

In 1972 he married Renate Ponsold, a German-born photographer who is best known for, but not limited to, making portarits of artists. (*Eye to Eye,* a collection of these portraits, accompanied by an essay by Dore Ashton, is forthcoming from Hudson Hills Press.) Using only available light and black and white film, her subjects are often caught in a spontaneous yet characteristic gesture, the image cropped tellingly so that a detail from their usual habitat acts as a framing device for the person, the artist's essence suddenly showing forth. Her choice of subject makes perfect sense in the light of an observation by Motherwell to the poet Frank O'Hara: "What better way to spend one's life than to have, as one's primary task, the insistence on integrity of feeling? No wonder others are fascinated by artists.''

Joel Meyerowitz

cover Provincetown Arts, *1988*

Squid Salad

12 oz. squid or octopus
in olive oil,
drained and chopped
12 oz. baby European shrimp,
canned, fresh, or frozen
12 oz. celery, chopped
3 tablespoons tarragon
vinegar, preferably
the Dessaux Fils brand
½ teaspoon dried tarragon
1½ lemons, juiced
2 tablespoons olive oil

In a bowl, mix the vinegar, oil, tarragon, and lemon juice. When the dressing is well blended, add the celery and mix, then add the squid and shrimp and mix thoroughly. Cover the salad and refrigerate it for at least one hour before serving. Serve on glass plates, with lettuce leaves as a base and parsley to decorate the top. This is an elegant and easy-to-prepare first course for dinner.

Stuffed Turkey

Turkey:

1 14-lb. turkey

Stuffing:

6 medium onions, chopped
3 garlic cloves, chopped
12 tablespoons
whipped butter
3 tablespoons summer savory
1 tablespoon sweet basil
1 teaspoon thyme
1½ cups celery leaves and
stalks, chopped
3 7-oz. packages all-purpose
cubed bread stuffing
1 cup hot water, or water
as needed
salt and pepper to taste

Eight-minute Gravy:

turkey giblets
3 packages Knorr-Swiss
Hunter Sauce mix
(1 ⅛-oz. size)
1 oz. European
dried mushrooms

Heat 6 tablespoons butter in a skillet. Add the onions and garlic and saute for 10 minutes. Add the celery, herbs, salt, and pepper, and saute 5 minutes more. Pour in the hot water and simmer 10 more minutes.

Place stuffing cubes in a large bowl. Stir in herb mixture and nuts. Mix well. Melt the remaining 6 tablespoons butter and add to this mixture. Stuff the turkey and place the remaining stuffing in a buttered crock, cover with foil, and bake along with the turkey. Preheat the oven to 350°. Bake the turkey, uncovered, at 300° for 4 hours.

Boil the giblets in water until tender, then chop them. Prepare the Hunter Sauce according to package directions and add the giblets and mushrooms to it. Serve in a sauceboat. Serves about 20.

Note: The Motherwells serve their traditional Thanksgiving turkey with lingonberries instead of cranberries. They also serve the stuffing as a vegetable. The moistness of the dressing doesn't change in cooking. "I happen to like it one the dry side," Motherwell adds, "not mushy."

"Beside the Sea No. 24," oil on Strathmore 5 ply rag paper

Southern Whiskey Cake

½ cup whipped sweet butter
8 oz. confectioners'
**   10-x sugar**
6 tablespoons Jack Daniels
**   bourbon whiskey**
5 large eggs, separated
¾ cup ground hazelnuts
¾ cup ground pecans
3 dozen lady fingers
**   (2 or 3 3-oz. packages)**
1 teaspoon whipped butter

Line a 9 × 5 × 3 loaf pan with wax paper. Butter it with the teaspoon of whipped butter. In a mixing bowl, cream together the ½ cup of butter and the sugar with an electric mixer. In a separate bowl, add the whiskey to the egg yolks and mix well so that the yolks are dissolved into the whiskey. Add the egg mixture to the butter-and-sugar mixture. Fold in the nuts. Beat the egg whites until stiff and carefully fold them in with a whisk or wooden spoon. Cover the bottom of the loaf pan with lady fingers, top side down. Cover with about a ½-inch layer of the cream mixture. Cover this with another layer of lady fingers and repeat the procedure until there are three layers of mixture and four of cake, ending with a layer of lady fingers. Cover the pan with foil and wrap. Refrigerate a minimum of 24 hours, 2 days if possible, so that the flavors have time to blend into the cake. Unmold onto a platter and serve cut in thin slices. Serves 8 to 10.

This rich dessert requires no cooking and will keep well in the refrigerator for several days.

Note: You can use 1½ cups of hazelnuts or pecans, instead of half and half, to vary the flavor. You can decorate with a whipped cream icing if desired.

Renate's Bittersweet Chocolate Mousse

6 large eggs, separated
3 3-oz. bars of Lindt extra bittersweet chocolate with vanilla, or any good quality bittersweet chocolate
5 tablespoons cold water
2 teaspoons dark rum (optional)

Break chocolate into small pieces and put in a heavy iron or enamel pan. Add water (and rum, if used) and stir constantly with a wooden spoon over very low heat until the chocolate melts. Remove pan from heat and carefully stir egg yolks into chocolate with a spoon. (Chocolate mixture should be warm, not hot, or the eggs will curdle.) Stir briskly until yolks are well mixed. Beat egg whites until very stiff. Carefully add egg-white mixture to the chocolate, taking care to fold the eggs into the chocolate with a spoon or whisk. Pour into a large glass bowl or into 8 small dessert bowls. Refrigerate for 6 hours before serving. Serves 8, and the entire thing can be prepared in about 20 minutes.

Note: This mousse, though very rich, may not be quite sweet enough for some. In this case, serve it with half a pint of heavy cream whipped with 4 tablespoons of sugar and a dash of vanilla or rum (or other flavoring).

Certain forms in nature are especially irregular, with a linear turbulence that yet is directional. The shoreline that follows the edges of a continent, a bolt of lightning across the sky, a river snaking through hilly terrain, a vein in the human hand, a branch of the bittersweet vine: such forms have a dynamic energy, curving and twisting as they move with urgency and excess from an imaginary point A to an imaginary point B. Susan Lyman is fascinated at the sculptural, volumetric, possibilities hidden in the energy of such lines. She recalls Paul Klee's definition of drawing as "taking a line for a walk," and she herself seems to think of sculpture as three-dimensional drawing.

Many of her constructions are skeletal. Using strong, flexible materials like reed and rattan, and more recently roots, branches, and vines, she fashions hollow, yet contained, spaces, suggesting cocoons and nests. Sometimes she covers them with a translucent skin, "at once revealing and hiding their underlying structure," she says, explaining, "these could be the vessels or miniature dwellings of an imaginary creature or body." Early in her career, shortly after receiving an MFA in ceramics from the University of Michigan, she made basket-like clay vessels, dipping yarn in wet clay, weaving the strands, then burning away the yarn during the firing in the kiln. The light that appears to come from within her filigreed forms gives her work an apparitional quality. She admits she has always been more interested in structures than in what covered them, and her work seeks to imply the ghost of that covering rather than the covering itself.

Recent work evolved out of her residency in Provincetown as a Fellow at The Fine Arts Work Center. Amid the company of many painters, she says, "I was greatly impressed by their ability to improvise, and I wanted to incorporate this flexibility into my own work." The daughter of an architect and the granddaughter of a well-known Michigan landscape architect, she had previously approached the making of art with the mind of an engineer, building predetermined forms as sketched. She now began to use a building process in her sculpture that was as organic as the branches and vines, fusing sections according to her own emotional impulses. "People Look Ridiculous When They're in Ecstasy" is an example of her ability to link man and nature through gestural metaphors, the branches remaining themselves yet standing for us.

Spicy-Hot Chicken

This recipe is adapted from an evening of shared cooking among Artists-in-Residence at Artpark in Lewiston, NY, in 1982. The other two recipes, for the most part, should be credited to my husband, Doug Trumbo, chief cook and bottle washer.

Chicken parts, or cut-up fryer, skin removed
sesame oil
4 to 5 garlic cloves, sliced
⅓ to ½ cup tamari
⅛ to ¼ cup honey
2 teaspoons dry mustard
crushed red pepper or Tabasco sauce, to taste

Saute the garlic in sesame oil in a skillet. Brown the chicken in the garlic-oil mixture. Mix the other ingredients to taste, pour them over chicken, cover the skillet, and cook over medium heat for half an hour, basting occasionally. Uncover and cook for 15 more minutes. Serve with rice.

Shrimp, Pesto, and Artichoke Pizza

Dough:
2 tablespoons fresh active yeast
⅔ cup warm water
a dash of salt
2 tablespoons cooking oil
1 cup white flour
1 cup whole wheat flour (or a total of 2 cups white flour)

Dissolve the yeast in the warm water. Add the salt and the oil. Add the flour (either half white and half whole wheat, or all white). Knead, let the dough rise in an oiled bowl covered with a damp cloth in a warm oven until its volume about doubles. Punch down and roll out the dough so it will fit a lightly oiled pizza pan, allowing enough to make a crust.

olive oil
⅓ cup pesto sauce
Cheddar cheese, medium or sharp, grated
mozzarella cheese, grated
1 lb. medium shrimp, peeled
1 can artichoke hearts, quartered

Preheat the oven to 450°. Sprinkle the rolled pizza dough generously with olive oil. Spread the pesto sauce over the dough and layer the cheeses on top, followed by the shrimp and artichoke hearts. Bake the pizza until the cheese bubbles and browns slightly.

Chicki-Guici

olive oil
1 chicken, cut up and breaded
4 garlic cloves, sliced thin
½ lb. linguica, sliced
1 large green pepper, sliced
1 large Bermuda onion, sliced
½ cup Marsala or white wine

Heat some olive oil in a heavy pan and brown the chicken pieces on one side. Turn once. Add the sliced garlic, linguica, green pepper, onion, and wine. Cover and simmer (or bake in the oven at 350°) for 45 minutes to an hour. Serves 4.

Foreground:
"Family Matters"
cherry, willow, privet, bittersweet vine

Background:
"People Look Ridiculous When They're in Ecstasy"
bittersweet vine, oil paint

Natalie Leimkuler

The idea that a picture is a moment in time implies a before and after, and therefore implies a story. Elspeth Halvorsen, who began her career as a painter, seeks in her box constructions to tell a story, only she chooses moments in time called "Primavera" or "Origin," large moments that already have been taken out of historical time and placed in poetic time. (Aristotle said that poetry was more philosophical than history because it universalized the particular moment.) Using

aluminum, mirrors and sand, she fashions spare landscapes, seen in cross-section as dioramas behind a pane of glass. Sheets of polished aluminum, curved like the deep sky at the far reaches of space where the universe curves back on itself, are set behind small mounds of sand, looking in scale as large as dunes on the moon seen through a powerful telescope. The image is suddenly, eerily, brought up close. Often she will cut apertures in the frames of her boxes, so that a small circle of cool light falls like a splash upon the smooth metal, setting off ripples of refractions. For many years she has spent part of every summer living with her husband in a shack on the dunes, one source of her inspiration. But she also spent winters in Indiana, where she has been witness to the sorry sight of flagrant strip-mining, leaving vast barren pits, and something of this geological sorrow inhabits her essentialized landscapes, which achieve a dignity of permanence at the cost of excluding man. Her favorite poet is William Butler Yeats, the artificer of eternity, "who," she says, "so often praises the moon and gives voice to the sea."

Tony Vevers was born in London, coming to the United States in 1940, when he was a teenager and he and his family were refugees from the Blitz. He attended Hotchkiss School where he discovered painting, then after service in the Army, he attended Yale University, majoring in painting and drawing. While studying and working in Florence for two years, he met Steve Pace and Larry Calagno, who introduced him to the issues of Abstract Expressionism. In the fall of 1952, Vevers returned to live in New York: "I found a loft studio on Delancey Street, hung out at the Cedar Bar, attended meetings at the Artists' Club and studied at Hofmann's School on 8th Street—it was a wonderful time to be a young painter." Two years later, he had met and married Elspeth Halvorsen. When their first daughter was born in 1955, they decided to leave

New York, settling in Provincetown at the encouragement of Fritz Bultman. Vever's response to Abstract Expressionism was to become increasingly figurative, and in Provincetown he found himself exhibiting at the legendary Sun Gallery, which had become the center for young figurative artists like Jan Muller, Alex Katz and Marcia Marcus. After years of working as a carpenter in Provincetown, Vevers began spending the academic year in Indiana where he taught painting, drawing and art history at Purdue University. In the early 70s he began to move from a figurative to an abstract approach, making pictures incorporating sand from the Wabash River. Some of these early works came from aerial photographs of the Wabash countryside. Large rectangular patches of muted sand colors, looking like a Vevers collage, lay flat on the canvas, peculiarly, as if the ground had shifted and the picture is seen from a bird's-eye view high above, where the sense of depth has been distorted due to the lack of intervening objects that ordinarily located perspective along the horizontal. Lately, Vevers has begun to extend his metaphor, using found objects and a limited return to the figure.

Tony's Meat Balls

When Miriam (Yum-Yum) Evans had her restaurant at 423 Commercial St., this recipe was a featured dish that was enjoyed by Myron Stout, among others, in those halcyon days of the late '50s.

1 onion, finely chopped
1 tablespoon oil
1 lb. ground beef
1 slice of bread,
  soaked in milk
1 egg, beaten
1 pinch nutmeg
flour
1 tablespoon vegetable oil
1 can beef bouillon
½ cabbage, shredded
½ teaspoon dill seed

Fry the onion in a little oil until golden. Mix well with the ground beef, bread, egg, and nutmeg. Form into ping-pong-sized balls. Dust the meat balls with flour and fry them in oil until they are brown on the outside (about 10 minutes). Remove them from the pan and keep them warm. Add the bouillon to the pan, and then the cabbage and the dill seed; place the meat balls on top and cover the pan. Cook over low heat for 20 minutes, until the cabbage is done to your taste. Serve with rye bread and butter.

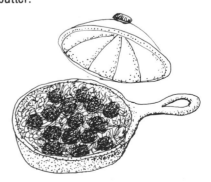

½ teaspoon sugar
1 tablespoon wine vinegar
1 tablespoon plain yogurt
1 tablespoon olive oil
1 garlic clove, minced

Mix the sugar and the vinegar. When the sugar is dissolved, mix in the yogurt. Pour in the olive oil and add the garlic to the oil. Let stand for a few minutes, then mix thoroughly. Pour over salad, toss, and serve. It's important to make this shortly before serving, since the garlic will become too strong if allowed to stand.

This is good with a flavorful lettuce, the kind you get in the winter. It will overpower a delicate leaf.

NOTE: Now that red sweet peppers are widely available, we have a fine alternative to those insipid tomatoes that the stores have inflicted on us for so long!

Tony Vevers, "Iphigenia"

Jagaçita—
Portuguese Paella

This was the first Portuguese recipe we tried when we came to Provincetown in the winter of 1955, and it is still our favorite. I offer it with a toast to Maurice Lopes, who was so helpful to us that winter and gave us the recipe after taking us on our first clamming expedition. It is the perfect dish for a cold winter night with your favorite guests. It can be made ahead of time and reheated in the oven while you prepare the garlic bread.

Elspeth Halvorsen

1 cup white rice
1 lb. linguica (Portuguese sausage) cut into ¼-inch slices
2 medium onions, sliced
1 red pepper, sliced
1 green pepper, sliced
2 or 3 chicken breasts, cut into bite-sized pieces
1 package tender tiny frozen peas, defrosted
1 dozen quahogs, or more

Cook the rice until the grains are light and separated. Meanwhile, in a large pan, fry the linguica, remove it, and set aside. Saute the onions and peppers in the remaining linguica fat. Brown the cut-up chicken in any remaining fat, adding a little cooking oil if necessary. Combine all these ingredients with the cooked rice. Add the clams and cover the pan. Cook gently until all the clams have opened. Add the peas and heat through. Serve with a hearty wine, a salad, and garlic bread. (For an appropriate salad dressing, see Tony Vevers's recipe.)

Elspeth Halvorsen, ink on paper

One of Sal Del Deo's favored views is of Long Point Light as seen from the little wharf that juts out in front of the second restaurant he started, Sal's Place, at the far west end of Provincetown, where the Cape tightens in its final spiral. Here, the faraway lighthouse seems suddenly brought close, as if magnified. This effect is translated in the layered seascapes and landscapes of Del Deo's paintings, which are often presented in circular or oval shapes against the rectangle of the canvas, as if the image were seen through a telescope or the oval of an eye with intensified vision. Within this aperture set within the frame, the painting, typically, shows horizontal stratifications of only several elements, sea, sky or shore. "The Cape is not a pretty place," he says, "but it is bleakly beautiful. Look how beach grass looks, growing in sand. Lower Cape landscape is especially interesting to an artist because it's not essentially anecdotal like, for instance, Rockport. There's an elemental quality, almost Japanese in feeling. The clouds here are turbulent, moving quickly, requiring the ability to catch them in a kind of sketch before they shift."

Perhaps the premier cook in town, Del Deo's cooking is like his painting, depending on the ability to make do, "*arrangiare,* as we say in Italian—to put your hand to something and make it work, even if you are all thumbs at first." He and Ciro Cozzi started Ciro and Sal's in 1953 as former Hensche students and struggling young artists preparing to cope with raising a family. According to Sal, "the partnership originated with the idea that I would be the cook because I always ended up cooking for fellow art students at parties, while

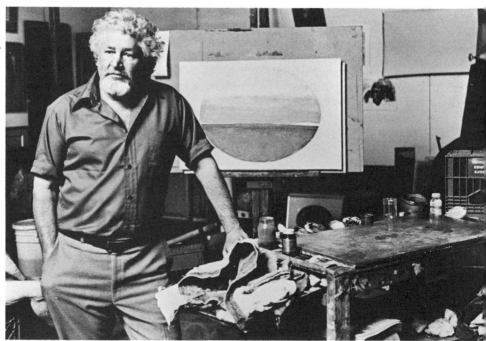

Gwendolyn Hobbs

Ciro would bring his restaurant experience to the enterprise." (According to the *Ciro and Sal's Cookbook*, "Ciro's restaurant experience consisted of stints as a waiter and dishwasher, both jobs at which he had not excelled.") They started by making Italian sandwiches and omelettes, and by the end of the first season, due to popular demand, they had worked in a few dishes of pasta, chicken and veal. "What happened in '53," Sal recalls, "was part miracle, part brass balls, and mostly necessity." Sinks for the new restaurant were made by Sal's father, Romolo, a coppersmith and tinsmith, who hammered tin to a plywood frame. When a solid floor was laid in the cellar dining room, in time for Sal's wedding reception, the cement was barely set, and the celebration, fueled with champagne and chianti, took place on a seemingly shaky foundation.

Today, retired from his successful restaurant, Del Deo paints full time. A son, Romolo, is a sculptor whose first art classes were taught by his father. A *summa cum laude* graduate of Harvard, where he "got the feeling that art history was moving in reverse," Romolo divides his time between the old world of Italy and the new world of New York, occasionally visiting Provincetown, as he did recently to show with his father in a unique father-son exhibition at the Cherry Stone Gallery. A daughter, Giovanna, a Williams graduate, also learned painting at her father's knee, and is now a free-lance writer and art agent in New York.

Fish Soup

heads of various white, firm-fleshed fish (not bluefish)
1 gallon water
½ cup olive oil
4 scallions, diced, or 1 small onion, finely chopped
leaves from 1 head of celery
3 or 4 potatoes, diced
sage, fresh if possible, chopped
black pepper, hand ground
salt, a pinch
¼ lb. butter
croutons (recipe follows)
1 cup chopped parsley

Clean the blood and scales off discarded fish heads to make the stock. Use haddock, bass, cod, cusk, and tautog. Place the fish heads in a large pot and cover with one gallon of cold water. Boil them until the meat begins to fall off the heads. Remove the heads and strain the broth through several layers of cheesecloth; set the stock aside. Remove all the meat from the fish heads (be careful of tiny bones) and reserve the meat.

Now, film the bottom of a fresh large sauce pot with olive oil. Add the diced scallions (or onions, finely chopped) and the celery leaves, and them let simmer on low heat for five minutes. Add the fish stock, and after a few minutes, when the broth is hot, add the diced potatoes, sage, black pepper to taste, and butter. Finally, add the fish meat and let the soup simmer until the potatoes are cooked (but not too soft). Serve the finished soup in large deep platter with homemade croutons and a sprinkle of chopped parsley.

Homemade Croutons

**French or Portuguese bread,
the best you can buy or
make (dried is best)**
olive oil
butter, melted
garlic powder
salt and pepper to taste

Dice the bread into ½-inch squares and place in a bowl. Add olive oil and melted butter (enough to moisten and flavor the bread), a little salt, black pepper, and garlic powder. Toss to mix, then spread the seasoned cubes out in a single layer in a baking pan and place them in a moderate oven. When they are toasted, remove them. They are now ready to serve. These may be kept in the refrigerator for several days.

Calamare Stufatto or Squid Stew

**squid, 8 to 10 inches long,
cleaned and cut into rings**
**½ cup olive oil, or more,
if needed**
1 bay leaf
**4 scallions or 1 small white
onion, chopped**
some celery leaves, chopped
1 large green pepper, diced
½ cup Burgundy red wine
½ cup dry sherry
salt and pepper to taste
**1 teaspoon red pepper flakes
or fresh hot peppers
when available**
1 teaspoon oregano
¼ lb. butter
**2 cups Italian tomatoes,
crushed, or use sugo
sauce if you have it**
½ cup Marsala

*If you want to make this simple
fare more elegant, add a
package of frozen shrimp when
you add the squid meats.*

To clean the squid: remove the insides and, with one motion, remove the bone. Grab the tentacles and cut just below the eye. Then pop out the little sacs (the mouth, or beak, and the ink sacs). Remove the two longest tentacles, as they are undesirable. Wash again, and if squid are inky, wash them until the meats are white. Cut the bodies crosswise, into rings. (If the squid are very large, you may cut them into strips.) Now set the meats aside and prepare the sauce.

Pour a film of olive oil into a sauce pot and place it over low heat. Add the bay leaf, the scallions or onion, the celery leaves, and green pepper. Let it simmer, being careful not to burn the oil (add more oil if the vegetables look too dry).

When the ingredients are getting "soft," add the squid rings and tentacles and stir vigorously until all are combined. Add the Burgundy and the sherry and let simmer a while longer. When the squid starts turning color, add salt, black pepper, red pepper flakes (or fresh hot peppers), oregano, and butter. Mix again and add 2 cups of sugo sauce or the canned tomatoes (hand-crushed). Finally, add the Marsala and stir all together. Let cook for about 15 minutes, or until the alcohol has evaporated. Serve as a main course, with pasta first, using the same sauce; but be sure to undercook the pasta.

Spaghetti alla Foriana

As a child, my mother prepared a special pasta with raisins and walnuts, herbs, anchovies or sardines, twice a year, on Good Friday and Christmas Eve. These high holy days were fast days, meaning no meat. Images of our "ancestral island" would float in my child's imagination as I dug deep into my dish for walnut pieces and raisins. Later in my student days I often times entertained my guests with a dish of my "Foriana Spaghetti." It was cheap to make and always surprised and pleased the palates of my friends. In 1953 Ciro Cozzi and I began our modest eating place and for the first time served this pasta with some hesitation, but to our surprise it became our most famous dish.

1 lb. of pasta, spaghetti or spaghettini (Italian or homemade)
8 anchovy fillets
1 cup of olive oil,
  the best you can buy
3 tablespoons salt, for
  the boiling pasta water
4 garlic cloves, chopped
1 bay leaf
½ cup chopped walnuts
¼ to ½ cup pine nuts
½ teaspoon oregano
1 cup raisins
½ dozen flakes red pepper or
  1 fresh hot pepper, chopped
black pepper, hand ground,
  to taste
½ cup chopped parsley

Pour the olive oil into a frying pan or skillet and set it over low heat. Add the bay leaf and the garlic. When the garlic starts bouncing about, add 4 anchovy fillets, moving them around with a wooden spoon. Stir well. Add the parsley and the oregano; stir again, and grind in some black pepper (my preference is to stop when you can see the black pepper dots on the surface of the skillet). Finally, add the hot red pepper, the chopped walnuts, and the pine nuts; stir once more, and last but not least, add the raisins. Stir all and let the sauce simmer over very low heat. Do not allow the raisins to burn.

Now to the cooking of the pasta: Pour a gallon of *cold* water into a large pot, cover and set over high heat. When the water starts to boil, add the salt, then add the pasta and cook at a rolling boil until it is *al dente*, that is to say, "firm to the bite." Fresh homemade pasta will cook very quickly, so you must be very attentive. Drain the pasta, but leave the drippings of the cooked pasta in the spaghetti pot to add to your sauce, if necessary. The pasta should be drained quickly and added to the sauce before it has a chance to stick together.

Combine the pasta and the sauce in the skillet or in a bowl, and serve hot. (Be sure that your guests are seated beforehand.) Place a fillet of anchovy on each mound of pasta and garnish with the chopped parsley. Serves 4.

"I want to be an artist," Cynthia Packard wrote in the diary she kept while a teenager, remembering the exact moment: "I was scared. *That* was a commitment! That meant that I could succeed or fail." Not yet 30, she has pursued her career with confidence and determination. She has exhibited in Boston at the Zoe Gallery on Newbury Street and in Provincetown at the East End, DeBerry, and, currently, at the new Anne Packard Gallery (a former Christian Scientist Church now owned by Cynthia's mother). During her recent pregnancy she painted with a gas mask so the fumes would not harm her unborn baby. An AAU black belt in karate and a former New England Woman's Champion, she stays in shape by training and teaching karate at the Provincetown Martial Arts School, run by her husband, Larry Luster.

A graduate of the Massachusetts College of Art, Cynthia was early exposed to art through her mother, Anne Packard. As a teenager, she modeled for the late Fritz Bultman, whose voluptuous, voluminous drawings are a celebrated aspect of his legacy. After modeling for him, Bultman asked her to draw with him, which she then did several times a

Cynthia Packard (l.) with her sister Leslie

week. "He was my mentor, my friend, my father," she said at the time of his death.

Cynthia's paintings are often of women in domestic spaces — bedrooms or kitchens. They appear to be talking, but their faces are featureless, their eyes and noses and mouths absent, replaced by an arbitrary color as in the evocative portraits by Milton Avery, whose paintings made her weep the first time she saw one. "What is color, line, shape, form?" she wondered about her own work, replying, "I ask these questions within the space of four edges. All the edges are connected and run continuously, never ending. The subject matter? Women reflecting. They are in an intimate interior where people can think and everything is still."

A Wonderful Omelette for Two

6 eggs, beaten
2 garlic cloves, crushed
1 tablespoon olive oil
½ lb. spinach
1 tablespoon sesame oil
1 tablespoon butter
4 oz. cream cheese
salt and pepper to taste

Saute the garlic in the olive oil. Steam the spinach. Then throw the spinach in with the garlic, toss it around, and top with sesame oil.

Melt the butter in a separate pan. Pour in the seasoned beaten eggs and cook on low heat with the cream cheese dabbled over the eggs. Then spread the spinach mixture over that, fold the omelette over, and serve with toast.

Rum Punch for Two

1 cup apricot nectar
1 cup pineapple juice
1 cup orange juice
½ cup cranberry juice
¾ cup Myers rum
a little Rose's Lime Juice

Combine all the ingredients and lots of ice in a pitcher and shake until foamy. Pour into glasses and garnish with fresh lime.

"Breakfast
Table"

Bill Barrell's painting is colorful and kooky, with shack-like shapes collapsing around stick figures, as in a child's fingerpainting of his house and family. If he describes his daughter's luminous wonder over a shell she has found on the beach—"her eyes became round, her jaw square, her hair stood on end, especially the eyebrows"—he also describes how his work expresses emotion through distortion. Something impish shines through Barrell's apparent innocence, since, like an inspired mimic, he plays off sources in Picasso, Rouault, and others. Like Dubuffet, he emphasizes his innocence by painting crudely in the service of making a good painting. It is the same with his cooking, his "Flake White Flounder," "Cadmium Red Chicken," and "Sausages Burnt Umber," invented as if for an artist's cookbook. Chef Bill hopes only that his spelling may be deciphered "so we do not give anybody indigestion."

Born in London to a father who was a chimney sweep, Barrell is a graduate of the school of hard knocks, doing menial jobs rather than going to school. When he was 22, he persuaded his entire family to move to the U.S., where he attended several art schools, including the Hans Hofmann class in Provincetown. Thirty years ago, he was among the younger generation of artists who were experimenting with figuration and turning away from abstract expressionism, which "had become too common and accepted to remain avant-garde," the critic Irving Sandler remarks in a memoir of the Sun Gallery, where Barrell exhibited, along with the other "neo-expressionists" of the day, including Red Grooms, Mimi Gross, Alex Katz, Jay Milder, and Tony Vevers. Barrell found that "the figure kept emerging in my work, even when I tried to paint abstractly." He recalls swimming in the bay and looking up at the houses built along the shore, the foundations in the sand, holding together at cockeyed angles. "By some magical means known only to P-town, I was transformed into an artist, and I have been grateful ever since. It was a relief to find something I could do that was invulnerable to criticism, that it didn't matter what people said. I find myself returning as often as possible to recharge my soul."

Flake White Flounder

1 lb. flounder fillets
¼ cup snow peas
2 small yellow squash, sliced
1 large broccoli stalk, cut
  into long thin pieces
2 tablespoons olive oil
¼ tablespoon sesame oil
½ teaspoon tarragon
¼ cup soy sauce and water,
  mixed fifty-fifty

Heat the olive and sesame oils in a small frying pan. Toss in the squash, broccoli, and snow peas. Stir-fry for five minutes. Reduce the heat and place the flounder fillets on top of the vegetables. Over this pour the mixture of soy sauce and water. Sprinkle tarragon on the fillets. Cover the pan and cook gently until the flounder is opaque and flakes easily. Serve with rice or new potatoes. A squeeze of lemon goes good with this dish. Serves two.

Sausages Burnt Umber (Toad in the Hole)

2 lbs. sweet Italian sausage
⅞ cup flour
½ teaspoon salt
½ cup milk
2 eggs, beaten
½ cup water
¼ cup corn oil

Preheat the oven to 400°. The ingredients for the batter must be at room temperature. Mix the flour and salt. Make a well in the center in which to pour ½ cup milk. Stir the mixture well. Beat the eggs until fluffy, then beat them into the batter. Add ½ cup water. Beat well until bubbles rise to the surface. Let stand. Meanwhile, cook the sausages (broil or pan fry). Place the sausages in a very hot pan (9 × 12 × 2, approximately), keeping them separated, and pour ¼ cup of hot corn oil over them. Now beat the batter one more time and pour over the sausages. Immediately place the dish in the oven, bake for 15 minutes, then reduce the heat to 350° and cook for another 10–15 minutes. This dish will puff up and take on some interesting sculptural shapes. Serve it with a green vegetable such as peas, broccoli, or asparagus. This dish is ready to go the minute it comes out of the oven, so have the rest of the meal ready and your guests seated at table, for maximum effect. The secret to this dish is to have the oil and the pan good and hot when placed in the oven.

12 chicken pieces,
  thighs and drumsticks
¼ cup olive oil
1 teaspoon sesame oil
4 large onions, sliced
1 large sweet red pepper,
  sliced into rings
1 lb. mushrooms, sliced
2 garlic cloves,
  peeled and chopped
¼ teaspoon hot pepper sauce
2 to 3 lbs. mussels, well
  scrubbed, beards removed
1 small green cabbage

Pour the olive oil and the sesame oil into a large (12-inch) skillet or frying pan. Saute the sliced onions, peppers, and mushrooms gently until the onions are transparent. Add one chopped garlic clove a few minutes before the end of sauteing. Remove the sauteed vegetables to a warm plate, leaving the oil in the pan.

Place the chicken pieces in the pan and gently brown them on both sides (five minutes). Reduce the heat. Place the onions, mushrooms, peppers, and garlic on top of the chicken pieces. Sprinkle on ¼ teaspoon hot pepper sauce. Place the cleaned uncooked mussels on top of the vegetables. Cut the cabbage in half and separate the leaves. Cover the mussels completely with cabbage leaves, curving the leaves downward. Cover the pan and simmer gently for 45 minutes. Feeds six collectors or four starving artists. Serve hot with plenty of garlic bread.

"Louisiana Houses," oil

Jim Zimmerman

Eighteen years ago, while a student at the Art Student's League in New York, Lois Griffel saw that her work was gray and dull, like the city, where the sunlight seldom shines on anything organic. She was told, "You have to go to Provincetown to paint color and landscape." And so she did, enrolling in Henry Hensche's classes. Hensche stressed the painting of color as it occurs in nature, where a red plant, examined closely, shows itself to be composed of many reds, side by side, commingling in variety as color that is "alive." Hensche's color theory, inherited from his mentor, Charles Hawthorne, recognizes the superior vividness in nature, and advocates a technique of placing "spots of color" side by side as a way of overcoming the uniform, uninflected artificiality of a flat coat of paint. Griffel returned to Provincetown summer after summer, painting in Hensche's outdoor classes, getting "bitten by mosquitos and burned by the sun," and absorbing Hensche's fierce dogma about the Impressionist way of seeing. "Look at what's happened to art since Hawthorne's death!" he declaims. "For 60,000 years artists have been striving for a clearer understanding of the visual world. With the Impressionists, logic finally triumphed. Painting began to become the science of seeing. But what happened? A few years after Monet's discoveries, realistic art is in retreat. And now all we see is one fashion after another, one theory after another—as if a great idea came along every month!"

In 1987, anticipating his retirement, Lois Griffel took over the building at 46 Pearl Street which housed his Cape School of Art. He said, "She will teach what she has learned, largely from me. I think she will do well, and I wish her well. I know she won't use the name in vain. What Lois and I are teaching here is something you won't get anywhere else in the country."

"Stream through the Pamet," oil on board

Palette-Pleasin'
Pea Soup

This is a classical recipe. The formula dates back from old master chefs. It is a dense, heavy, rich mixture, usually stirred in dark corners of north light kitchens. It has recently been enhanced by the quality of color-balanced, natural lighting, and also by brilliantly colored vegetables grown directly outdoors.

1 tablespoon butter
1 cup onion, chopped
1 cup carrots, sliced
½ cup celery, chopped
1 ham bone
1 lb. dried green split peas
1 12-oz. can beer
4 cups water
1 bay leaf
¼ teaspoon dried leaf thyme
1 tablespoon vinegar
1 teaspoon salt
Tabasco to taste

Melt the butter in a large pot. Add the onion, carrots, and celery, and cook until soft. Add the ham bone, peas, beer, water, bay leaf, thyme, vinegar, salt, and Tabasco. Cover and bring to a boil. Reduce the heat and skim any foam fr⌐ the top of the pot. Simmer the sou⌐ two hours.

Remove the ham bone, shred⌐ meat, and reserve it. Discard⌐ and the bay leaf. Puree th⌐ small batches, in a proc⌐ smooth. Return it to t' if the soup is too th⌐ meat. Simmer fiv⌐ serve. Serves ⌐

Super-rich, Super-intense Highly-saturated Carrot Cake

2 cups Titanium White flour
2 teaspoons Flake White baking soda
2 teaspoons Flake White baking powder
2 cups pure, white sugar (non-yellowing)
3 eggs (Cadmium Yellow deep yolks only)
¾ cup mayonnaise (may have a touch of Indian Yellow)
8 oz. pineapple (either Cadmium Lemon or Cadmium Yellow light), crushed
4 cups carrots, finely grated (Cadmium Orange a must!),
1 or 2 teaspoons vanilla extract (not vanilla colored at all, but really Sienna)
1 teaspoon salt (any pure pigmentation will do)
2 teaspoons cinnamon (color varies from Venetian Red to Mars Orange)

Sift the flour, soda, baking powder, salt, sugar, and cinnamon into a bowl. (I use a beautiful turquoise ceramic bowl; use your imagination!) Stir in the mayonnaise gradually, and add the eggs one at a time. (I use a large palette knife for this.) Mix well: there should be no striations in the color.

Add the drained crushed pineapple, and last, stir in the carrots and the vanilla extract. Pour the batter into a greased and floured Bundt pan. Bake the cake slowly, at 350°, for 45-60 minutes, until done.

Let the cake cool and frost with cream cheese icing:

Icing
(non-oily variety)

k butter
s confectioner's

cheese, softened
vanilla extract

Cream the butter and sugar, using short, light strokes. Stir in the cream cheese. Beat until the mixture is spreadable with a small palette knife. Add the vanilla extract. Frost the cake when it has cooled.

What kind of food does a gritty sensualist eat? Ask Jim Peters, a gritty sensualist, known for large, multi-media paintings usually of interior cutaways showing some scene from the private life of a pair of lovers. His personal history, like the windings of an intestine, wanders with organic logic from the mess halls of Annapolis to a masters degree in nuclear engineering from MIT, takes a turn deep in the bowels of an aircraft carrier, before abruptly snaking back to the Annapolis area when Peters attends the Maryland Institute of Art. One morning while lying in bed in Connecticut, at a decisive moment in consideration of his brilliant career in the Navy which had sent him to MIT on full scholarship, the thought came into Peters' head, "Hey, I can be an artist." On very little evidence, he was accepted at the Maryland Institute, where he earned an MFA, making him one of the few artists with masters degrees in both science and art. Living in suburban Connecticut, he radicalized sleepy communities with 60s-style performance pieces. Often he dressed in costumes. In Connecticut, Peters met Vicky Tomayko. Three days later, talking on the phone, they agreed to walk the railroad tracks that connected their two homes, meeting halfway. Both were accepted as fellows at the Fine Arts Work Center, where Jim currently serves on the staff as chairman of the visual committee. In 1985 Peters was selected as one of nine artists nationwide to show in New York at the Guggenheim Museum exhibition "New Horizons in American Art."

In his Provincetown studio, Peters dips his coarse brushes into dark paint, touches brush to canvas (often he paints instead on tin, glass, wood or refrigerator door), and, smearing the brush, soils the perfect flesh of his ideal woman (the facial expression is consistently flattened out, slack as the facial muscles of a person in a trance). As Renaissance painters again and again painted the image of Christ, so Peters returns to his iconographic female, a kind of Brigitte Bardot without her hot pants, whom he regards as

"confrontative and tough," caught dreaming in some drab domestic space such as an unmade bed or a bathroom with all the plumbing exposed. The nooks and crannies of narrow rooms in Provincetown apartments, where a dormer will crowd down upon the living space, remind Peters of "industrially cozy" spaces deep inside Navy ships, where many men live less with women than with their imaginations of women. Perhaps, as Peters says, "the woman is the hero of my paintings," because it is her presence that makes romantic what would otherwise be rather severely spartan.

Vicky Tomayko's work consists of colorful and playful constructions, often boxes or shelves, which she attaches to the wall. Tiny animals, single letters, or round faces are tucked into apertures cut into her boxes, suggesting miniature theaters. 'If someone bought an empty one," she says, "perhaps they could put something in it for themselves." She considers that her constructions are shrinelike and are created to honor objects. Her actual studio, unlike Peters', is at home, doubling as a playroom for their toddler. "When Arvid makes a line," she says, "it is for the pure joy of making the line, the sheer joy of the color. That's what I want to learn from him — how to be pure." Occasionally, Tomayko will present her work in installations, creating a space in a gallery that simulates her studio/playroom at home, including familiar "little home things" that are not meant to be art (when they are exhibited, the gallery puts no price tag on them).

At home, while the chicken pie cooks in the oven, Jim is likely to prepare his special popcorn, praising it as nutritious, cheap, abundant, delicious, filling and gritty.

Chicken Pie

1 cup unbleached white flour
1 cup whole wheat flour
12 tablespoons margarine, cold, cut into pieces
5 tablespoons cold water
2 chicken breasts
4 tablespoons flour
1 tablespoon tarragon
cooking oil for stir-frying
2 cups apple juice
2 cups vegetables, diced (carrots, potatoes, peas, and/or green beans)
salt and pepper to taste

Have ready a pie pan. Mix together for a double crust the flours and the margarine. Use your fingers to lightly work margarine into the flour until pea-size pieces remain. Sprinkle with the water and gather the dough into a neat ball. Handling as little as possible, roll half of the dough out on a lightly floured cloth with a floured rolling pin. Fold into the pie pan and set aside.

Filling: Preheat the oven to 375°. Skin and bone the chicken breasts and cut them into bite-size pieces. Mix together in a bag the four tablespoons of flour and the tarragon. Add the chicken pieces and shake to coat. Heat a small amount of cooking oil in a large skillet or wok, and add the entire contents of the bag. Saute the chicken for five minutes, or until it is slightly browned, being careful not to burn the flour. Add the apple juice and cook for about another five minutes,

the bear saw a piece of pie and was glad.

stirring frequently, until the sauce is nicely thickened. Remove the pan from the heat. Mix in the diced vegetables and season to taste. Pour this mixture into the lined pan. Roll out a top crust from the remaining dough. To insure a good seal at the edge and to keep the juices from escaping, fold the top crust under the bottom crust (or lightly brush the rim of the bottom crust with cold water before putting on the top), and then press it down with a fork. Prick the top with a fork to allow steam to escape. Bake in a 375° oven for one hour. Cool a little before serving.

Vicky Tomayko, Installation,
East End Gallery, Provincetown, 1987

Popcorn

1 tablespoon olive oil
1 tablespoon corn oil
½ cup popping corn
2 oz. butter (optional)

The corn: The best stuff is co-op or healthfood store popping corn (actually tastes like corn!!). Next to that I like the cheapest A & P-type corn, "BANG-O," etc. "Jolly Time" used to be almost as good as co-op but has declined in quality the last five years. "Orville Reddenbacher's" is horrible. Sure it all pops, but has no zip, zero taste; might as well heat up pre-popped stuff.

The pan: This is the most important item other than the corn. In 30 years of popping, the best I've found is the bottom of an old pressure cooker (thick cast Al). Electric poppers aren't too bad, but it's like using an electric fry pan instead of a seasoned cast-iron skillet. Air poppers are for yuppies and air heads. No oil!! A sin to good popcorn production. *Important!!* Remember never to wash the pan immediately prior to use. Residual water vapor reduces the efficiency and crispness of the popping process.

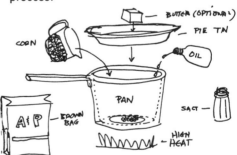

The oil: I mostly use pure corn oil. However, I often use pure olive oil or half olive and half corn oil. The olive oil brings a delightful flavor to the corn. Using corn oil is slightly incestuous I admit (like the relationship of linseed oil to linen). If you aren't into this try peanut oil.

The seasoning: Just use a little salt. This allows for maximum intake. Butter and brewer's yeast are good additives, but seriously limit the amount of corn you can ingest.

OK. *Let's go!* Place a 4-quart pan on high flame, add one tablespoon of olive oil and one tablespoon corn oil. Immediately add half a cup of popping corn. Cover with a tin pie plate. (The pie plate allows a loose fit for moisture release, corn expansion above pan top, and a reservoir for decadent butter.) When the popping stops or slows down considerably, immediately remove the popcorn from heat, dump it into an A & P brown bag (check for cleanness), add salt (the optional butter should be added before salt, if used), shake and eat.

Jim Peters,
"Movietime: Life Prevails," oil on canvas

Gillian Drake

If the term "still life" is understood as an opportunity to view objects suspended in a moment of time, surrounded by time, yet timeless on the occasion of their presentation, then Judith Shahn's subject is still life. In the many small drawings that have been appearing regularly in *The New Yorker* since the late 50s and in her numerous editions of silkscreen prints, which she began producing in order to make her work affordable to people who couldn't afford her paintings, she most often will isolate a single object, such as an old handcrafted chair sitting in white space, and depict it with an eye for its intrinsic character. In one silkscreen she casts the shadows of three flatbottomed boats onto a blue background, so that the boats themselves, floating on their shadows, have a reality as intensely compelling as apparitions. Her drawings of porches and windows, flowers and fruit, and especially the many odd appliances found in the kitchen of a devoted cook, such as a hand-driven eggbeater, are at once homespun and sophisticated. They radiate the charm that is the celebrated essence of *The New Yorker*, with its anachronistic insistence on quality, on poetry that is at least as well written as prose and on drawing that is least as aptly executed as illustration.

Judith Shahn was born in Paris in 1929 on Bastille Day. The next year, her father, the painter Ben Shahn, would return to the United States and alter his painting after being moved by the case of Sacco and Vanzetti, the anarchists who sold fish, repaired shoes, and were executed because a judge didn't like Italians. The power of the artist to affect cultural values is sometimes acknowledged grudgingly by way of praise for the passion of his message, but Ben Shahn defended the artist's engagement with social reality, saying, "I prefer to call it personal realism. The distinction is that social realism is dictated from the outside; personal realism comes from your own guts." Growing up during the Depression, then World War II, Judith Shahn absorbed the esthetic of immediacy in documentary photography and art made for public murals, protest posters, newspapers and magazines. She attended schools in New York City and graduated from Mexico City College in Mexico. While visiting with her mother who worked at the WPA's Index of American Design, whose task it was to document early American folk art, pottery, weavings, producing extremely accurate renderings of these objects, rather than photographs, Judith became impressed with the devotion behind the idea of representing with accuracy the real. "Reaching maturity at a time when MFA programs were few," she says, "and grants for emerging artists virtually non-existent, for many years I had a series of unrelated jobs." One of these included an unsuccessful foray into the business world. She, her husband, the poet Alan Dugan, and another couple tried to make ends meet by setting up a small greeting card company. "All this in an effort to support myself while I kept on painting: nights, weekends, during vacations, between jobs." When the prices of her paintings began going up, she thought, "I don't want to be selling only to the rich," and began making silkscreens in editions of 100, so that they could be priced reasonably. She says that she takes "real pleasure" in the fact that often the first piece of "real art" that a young couple or a young person wants to buy is one of her prints.

A hard worker and a prolific artist who has had more than 40 solo shows in places ranging from New York to Rome to California, she returns regularly to the Truro, where she does all her own printing, presently in a new studio attached to a house her parents bought before she was born. Like many artists, she has long had a great interest in food and cooking. In particular she is grateful to her mother who never urged cooking upon her as an activity appropriate to a female, but frequently told her that all good artists were good cooks, reminding her that her father too was an excellent cook.

On the Lower Cape, she and Dugan have been especially instrumental in creating a community of feeling for the Fine Arts Work Center, serving respectively on the visual and writing committees, reviewing slides and manuscripts, serving on the Board of Trustees, and meeting informally with Work Center Fellows.

FINE ARTS WORK CENTER IN PROVINCETOWN 1968-1988

Silkscreen print to commemorate the 20th anniversary of the Fine Arts Work Center in Provincetown.

Caldo Gallego

This is a version of a soup from Galicia, the most northwesterly province of Spain, which shares a border with Portugal. It is similar to the more familiar Portuguese kale soup.

3 large potatoes, peeled and cubed
1 yellow onion, chopped
¼ lb. ham, cubed (see note)
1 quart water or meat stock
1 19-oz. can garbanzos (chickpeas)
1 19-oz. can cannellini (white kidney beans)
½ lb. linguica or chourizo
1 10 oz. package frozen chopped spinach

Add the peeled cubed potatoes, chopped onion, and cubed ham to the water or stock. Boil until the potatoes are almost tender. Peel the linguica or chourizo, slice it into ¼-inch rounds, and add to the soup. Return to the boil. Add the can of chickpeas and the can of cannellini (do not drain) to the soup and return to a simmer.

Just before serving, add the frozen (or thawed) spinach to the soup. Heat just until the frozen spinach thaws, or the soup returns to a boil, and serve while the spinach is still bright green.

This amount will make 6 to 8 servings. The quantities can be multiplied to serve many more.

Note: If you have a hunk of leftover ham, this is a good way to use it. The water in which ham has been boiled makes the ideal stock for this soup. Or you can use a couple of smoked ham hocks; if you start with the hocks, boil them for about an hour, until tender; separate the meat from the bones, skin, and gristle, dice the meat, and return it to the broth before proceeding with the rest of the recipe. Or you can use a ¼ lb. chunk of deli boiled ham cut into ¼-inch cubes (not sliced).

Corn Pudding

4 cups fresh corn, cut off the cob
1 large yellow onion
2 tablespoons butter, plus butter to grease a baking dish
2 eggs
1 cup half-and-half (or ½ cup heavy cream and ½ cup milk)
½ green pepper, minced
½ sweet red pepper, minced
salt and freshly ground black pepper to taste

Preheat oven to 400°. Generously butter the bottom and sides of a 2-quart souffle or other baking dish. Finely chop half the onion and saute it in butter. Put 1 cup of the corn kernels and the other half of the onion into a food processor or blender. Process until finely pureed, then add the eggs and the half-and-half and blend well. Combine all the ingredients, add salt to taste, and lots of freshly ground black pepper. Mix well, pour into a buttered souffle or other baking dish, and bake for half an hour, or until the pudding starts to firm up and is lightly browned on top. Serve immediately.

Insalata di Frutti di Mare (Seafood Salad)

3 dozen mussels
1 lb. scallops
1 lb. medium shrimp
1 lb. squid
1 lb. monkfish (or other
firm-fleshed fish)
1 cup dry white wine
3 garlic cloves, crushed
1 red onion
1 yellow onion
1 teaspoon coarse (kosher)
salt
1 sweet red pepper
1 sweet green pepper
3 stalks celery
¾ cup plus ¼ cup lemon or
lime juice
½ cup sherry vinegar
1 cup good quality olive oil
(extra virgin, if possible)
1 tablespoon fresh herbs
(such as basil, dill,
summer savory, thyme,
chervil, etc.), minced

*Any combination of firm-fleshed fish
and shellfish can be used for this dish.
Also, the proportions of any of the
ingredients can be varied to taste.*

**Refer to pages 36 or 105 for
instructions on cleaning squid.*

Make the dressing: Crush 3 garlic cloves
with the coarse salt. In a tightly lidded
jar, mix the garlic with ¼ cup lemon
juice, ½ cup sherry vinegar, and one cup
of olive oil. Add your choice of minced
fresh herbs, and shake the jar vigorously
until its contents are well blended.

Rinse the scallops. If you are using
small bay scallops, leave them whole.
Cut large sea scallops, into halves or
quarters. Macerate them in a bowl with
the ¾ cup lemon or lime juice and
refrigerate for one hour or more, tossing
a couple of times, until the scallops
become opaque.

Scrub the mussels well. Place them in
a large pot (with a tight-fitting lid) with
one minced garlic clove, the chopped
yellow onion, and one cup of white wine.
Steam until the mussels open. Drain
them and save every drop of mussel
broth. Remove the mussels from their
shells (discarding any that have not
opened), and mix them with the dressing
in a large bowl. Cover and refrigerate.

Shell and devein the shrimp. Bring the
mussel broth to a full boil and drop the
shrimp in, stirring to make sure all the
shrimp make contact with boiling broth.
Cook for only a minute or so, just until
the shrimp are pink and opaque. Drain
the shrimp, once again saving every drop
of the broth. Mix the shrimp with the
mussels and the dressing mixture, and
refrigerate.

Clean the squid thoroughly. If
purchased, they will be fairly clean; but if
caught by you or a gift from a fishing
friend, find good instructions for cleaning
squid.* Cut off the tentacles and cut
them into one-inch lengths, and slice the
bodies into ¼-inch rings. Bring the
mussel liquor to a boil again, adding
more water if necessary. Drop in the
squid pieces, and leave them in only until
the liquid returns to the boil. Drain the

squid thoroughly, mix with other seafood, and refrigerate.

Cut the monkfish into pieces about one-inch square. Bring the mussel broth to a boil again. Once again add some water if necessary. Cook the monkfish in boiling broth very briefly, only until the fish is opaque. Drain the fish, toss it lightly with the other cooked ingredients, and refrigerate. (Save the cooking liquid for another dish. It can form the stock for a wonderful soup or chowder, and it will keep in the freezer.)

Cut the red onion, sweet green pepper, and sweet red pepper into thin strips. Dice the celery stalks. Mix the vegetables with the seafood mixture. Drain the scallops and toss them with the rest of the mixture. Refrigerate several hours or overnight, tossing occasionally. Taste to see if more salt is needed (it probably won't be), and add more if so desired.

This salad can be served on top of or accompanied by a tossed green leafy salad, with Portuguese or French bread (or garlic bread). It will serve 10 to 12 as a first course, or fewer people as a main course.

Midje Dolma
(Stuffed Mussels)

6 dozen mussels
   (the larger the better)
1 cup white wine
2 garlic cloves, minced
2 shallots, minced
2 yellow onions, chopped
½ cup parsley, chopped
½ cup olive oil
1½ cups converted rice
2 teaspoons dried mint or
   2 tablespoons fresh mint,
   chopped
½ cup dried currants
¾ cup pine nuts
¼ teaspoon ground nutmeg
salt, if necessary
lemons for garnish

Scrub the mussels well, scraping if necessary, and pull out mussel beards. Put the mussels in a large pot with a tightly fitting lid and add one cup of white wine, one minced garlic clove, one minced shallot, one chopped yellow onion, and the chopped parsley. Cover tightly and steam until the mussels open. Drain the mussels, reserving the broth. When the mussels are cool enough to handle, remove them from their shells and reserve both mussels and shells.

Add enough water to the mussel broth to measure 3 cups, and bring this liquid to a boil. Taste to see if more salt is required, and add some if needed.

Meanwhile, pour ½ cup olive oil into a

large skillet. Over medium low heat, stir in the remaining minced garlic clove, minced shallot, and finely chopped onion. Stirring frequently, saute until the onion is transparent. Add the rice and stir until it is well coated with olive oil and mixed with the vegetables. Do not let the rice brown. Add the boiling mussel broth all at once, cover the skillet tightly, and turn the heat to very low. After 15 minutes, add the pine nuts and the currants, stirring well. If the liquid has all been absorbed, cover the skillet, remove it from the heat, and let it sit, covered, for 5 to 10 minutes. If the liquid has not been absorbed, continue cooking over very low heat until it has been.

Place the rice mixture in a large bowl and add the mint and the nutmeg; toss well. If it seems a little dry, add a little more olive oil. When the rice mixture is cool enough to handle, line up the dish with the mussels, the bowl with the rice mixture, the container with the mussel shells, and an empty platter or serving dish. With your hands, stuff each pair of mussel shells with a mussel and some of the rice mixture. Force the shells closed. Your hands will get oily from handling the rice; wipe each stuffed mussel with oily hands until it is nice and shiny. Arrange stuffed mussels on platter. Cover and refrigerate.

Serve the stuffed mussels chilled, garnished with plenty of lemon wedges.

I much enjoyed the stuffed mussels (Midje Dolma) served at Armenian restaurants, and when mussels were still plentiful in the Pamet I experimented with ways to reproduce the subtle tastes and textures of the original. The recipe here is the approximation I came up with. I used to say that heaven would be the place where Midje Dolma were plentiful. One spring day in Izmir, Turkey, Dugan and I were sitting at an outdoor cafe, the streets filled with vendors of stuffed mussels, the large trays held high, laden with the delicacies which they sold for a dime. I sighed, "I must have died, and this is heaven."

Ray Elman is a graduate of the Wharton School of Finance at the University of Pennsylvania, where he also took a minor in fine arts. He recalls, "I began leading a schizophrenic existence. I would go to the Wharton School in a suit and tie with my attache case, attend class, leave the class, run over to the art studios, throw a lab coat over my suit and try not to get paint on my pants." After graduation, he worked on Wall Street for two years. Evenings, he took studio courses at New York University, where he met the painter Knox Martin, who taught him composition through the use of a grid. Elman recalls that Martin "made me understand ideas and feelings about painting which had just been words before, words like *plasticity*." In his early large canvases, he found that using the grid allowed him to create dynamic, unconsidered encounters, where "everything would relate to any part without my having to think about it. I finally found that I could paint two entirely separate paintings, bolt them together, and find they worked together, even if the sizes were different."

Leaving New York in 1970, Elman grew a beard and moved to Provincetown, living yearround for 15 years in a house on Mayflower Heights. With a constant view of the dunes sloping into Pilgrim Lake, he was able to watch the dunes "walk" toward him at the pace of three feet a year. The ghost of the previous owner, who had enjoyed the company of women with dangerous professions, inhabited the house, whose second floor had been cut away, leaving an open space that soared 35 feet, created so that the owner's girlfriend, a trapeze artist with the Ringling Brothers Circus, could stay in shape while she visited the Cape. Elman painted in this area. Deriving his abstract images from medieval and tantric symbols, he found his philosophy in a quotation that stayed pinned to his studio wall for many years: "Geometry is the plane between the physical world and the world of essential being." For several winters he helped run the *To Be Coffeehouse*, making brown food for essential beings with actual stomachs. The regulars ate lentil soup, whole wheat bread, Oriental vegetables in tamari, brown rice, and Brown Betty, washing it down with a thick apple cider, warm and flavored with cinnamon.

Currently Elman lives half of the year in Truro and half of the year in East Boston, on the top floor of a former New England Telephone Company building, now an artists' cooperative divided into lofts. (He shares the building with Stony Conley, Mary Armstrong, Diane Shumway and Peter Plamondon, each one of whom exhibits in Provincetown.) In his recent painting, Elman has returned to figuration, depicting large heads transfigured with tribal markings. Sometimes the large heads rest on small shoulders, clothed in the striped shirts, herringbone suits and polka dotted ties of the capitalist businessman. Sometimes the emphasis exaggerates as in the manner of cartoons, and indeed Elman values whatever humor people find in his long series of paintings called "Urban Masks." By painting big lips in bow ties, he suggests an identity between the cosmetic and the symbolic, the costumes of corporate man and the ritual expressions of primitive masks.

With his capacity to sense form amid jarring disjunctions, Elman has the negative capability that is the essential qualification for being an editor of an art magazine. In 1985 he and Christopher Busa founded *Provincetown Arts*, which has since grown into a comprehensive cultural magazine and which is undergoing expansion in conjunction with another company, USA Arts, Inc., with publishing ventures forthcoming in Cincinnati and Boston.

When he is aproned in his kitchen making re-fried beans and gambas a la plancha, two of his specialties shared by many of his many dinner guests, his wife, Lee Skye, a gourmet cook whose recipe for creme brulee is also included in this book, entertains in the living room, assuring the concerned that the clatter of pots and pans is not the creation of an Edsel, but the preparation of a meal. When the apron is ready for the laundry, the meal is ready. "I never met a good artist who wasn't a good cook," he says. "Artists have a strong sense of proportion, color and texture, but I finally decided they were good cooks mostly because they didn't mind getting messy."

"Urban Mask: Lunch in the Combat Zone"

Ray's Famous Original Refried Beans

I borrowed this recipe from an itinerant drummer I met in a recording studio in Cincinnati.

4 8-oz. cans or 2 cups dried kidney beans, thoroughly cooked
7 garlic cloves, squeezed through a press
1 4-oz. can Old El Paso taco sauce
safflower oil or any other light oil
salt and pepper to taste
jalapeno peppers, sliced

Take half of the beans, place them in a colander, and rinse off any excess cooking liquid, especially the liquid packed in the cans. Cover a deep cast-iron frying pan (or other heavy-duty pan; one 14 by 2 to 3 inches deep is ideal) with ¼ inch of oil. Heat over a high flame until the oil is hot. The flame must remain high until the dish is almost done. Add the garlic and saute until golden. Add the beans from the colander, cover the frying pan, and cook until the sides of the beans split (approximately 3 to 5 minutes).

Meanwhile, place the second half of the beans in the colander and rinse off any excess cooking liquid.

Be prepared: here comes the most awkward moment in refried-bean making! When the sides have split on the first batch of beans, remove the frying pan from the flame and, using slotted spoons, pour off as much excess oil as possible. I always seek help for this process, although I can go it alone if necessary. You can drain the oil into one of the empty bean cans (pre-rinsed) and save it for another load.

Return the pan to the flame and add the second batch of beans. Mix the new beans and the old beans, cover, and cook for approximately 2 or 3 minutes, stirring occasionally. Remove the cover, reduce the heat to low, and stir in the taco sauce, as well as salt and pepper to taste. Stir well and allow the mixture, to simmer for less than a minute. Mash with a potato masher. I prefer "refries" with texture, rather than as a puree. Texture is best achieved with a wide-grid potato masher. When the mashing is over, the beans are ready to serve.

Serves 4 to 8 persons, depending on whether you offer this dish as an appetizer or an entree.

Serving Suggestions:

1. Place the beans in a bowl, cover the top with a mixture of grated Cheddar and Monterey Jack cheeses, and place sliced jalapeno peppers on top. The hot beans will melt the cheese. Serve with tortilla chips.

2. Place the beans in a bowl and provide separate bowls of cheese, peppers, and chips, and allow your guests to make their own nachos.

3. Make bean burritos. Buy several packages of flour tortillas. Provide a square of aluminum foil for each burrito. Place the tortilla on the foil, add a dollop of beans, a few slices of jalapeno pepper, and a sprinkle of cheese. Roll the tortilla over the mixture and seal it with the foil. Bake the burritos for 5 minutes in a 450⁰ oven, or freeze the burritos for serving at a later date.

Gambas a la Plancha

Anybody who knows me well knows that this is my poor imitation of a dish served at El Charro in New York City.

32 medium- or jumbo-sized shrimp (in the shell)
3 tablespoons olive oil
5 garlic cloves, squeezed through a press
1 jalapeno pepper, chopped
handful of chopped parsley
juice of one lemon
⅓ cup dry white wine
4 tablespoons dry sherry
1 4 oz.-can of Old El Paso taco sauce
paprika

Use a wok or a deep frying pan that will fit under your broiler. Over a medium burner flame, heat the pan and add the olive oil. Add the crushed garlic and saute for one minute. Add the jalapeno pepper and continue to saute until the garlic is golden. Add the parsley, stirring continuously. Add the shrimp, continue stirring for 20 seconds, then add the lemon juice, taco sauce, sherry, and white wine. Cover the entire mixture with a liberal sprinkling of paprika, then put a lid on the pan. Cook for exactly 2 minutes, remove the lid, and place the pan under the broiler. Cook for another 2 minutes, and it's done. Serve over saffron rice.
    Serves 4.

Lee's Creme Brulee

This recipe was stolen from my wife, Lee Skye.

1 quart heavy cream
1 dozen egg yolks
3 oz. sugar
2 oz. liqueur of choice
(e.g., Frangelica, Grand
Marnier, Kahlua)

Topping:
½ cup brown sugar
½ cup white sugar

Preheat oven to 375°
10 6-oz. ramekins

Heat the cream over a medium flame in a 2-quart sauce pan until it is hot, BUT DO NOT BOIL. Set aside until cool. Thoroughly mix the sugar and the eggs until the sugar is dissolved. Continue stirring and pour the cooled cream into the sugar and egg mixture. Strain this mixture into 6-oz. ramekins. Place the ramekins in a *bain marie* (place ramekins in a baking pan and add water to the pan until the water is approximately halfway up the sides of the ramekins). In an oven that has been preheated to 375°, bake the custard for approximately 25 minutes, or until it is firm. Take the *bain marie* from the oven, remove the ramekins from the *bain marie*, and allow them to cool.

Thoroughly mix the brown and white sugars in a bowl and sprinkle the mixture over the top of each ramekin. Place the ramekins under a broiler and broil the topping until it turns brown and bubbles. Be careful not to burn it.

Remove from the broiler. As the topping cools, the sugar will caramelize and harden. Serves 10.

Serving Notes: Once the ramekins have been removed from the oven, I prefer to refrigerate the creme brulee prior to adding the topping, adding and broiling the topping just before serving. Thus the creme brulee is cool, while the topping is warm.

Summering at Sandy Neck off Barnstable, living in a cottage without hot water or electricity, obliged to take a boat when she wanted to get to town, Anne Packard began painting on small pieces of driftwood she found on the isolated beaches. At the time, she was 30, the mother of five children, married to a writer and teacher. In the winter she lived in New Jersey and worked for a catering company. She remembers, "I didn't paint. I cooked instead, and used the same energy that I now put into my painting." After a divorce and the disappearance of a son who was hiking in the California mountains, she began to paint in earnest, desperate to earn a living. In the same way that nobody except a blockhead writes except for money, she painted more from a need for money than to express herself, a motivation that has haunted her phenomenal success as one of Provincetown's best-selling seascape painters, with a following of collectors including Robert Redford, Eric Severeid, and Robert Motherwell, an East End neighbor. Motherwell began buying her small oils of the sky and sea after wandering by and seeing them hung like underwear on a clothesline for the summer traffic. Intense and atmospherically emotional, the paintings reminded Motherwell of a compacted Turner, the English Romantic who once had himself strapped to the mast of a ship during a snowstorm so that he could experience the turbulence from within. Similarly, Packard's paintings are about being within an experience that is removed from the viewer. Lacking formal organization, they achieve a coherence through a heightened luminosity in which even the most serene moment is depicted as though it were about to dissolve into a sublime chaos.

Packard is the granddaughter of the American Impressionist Max Bohm, who counselled, "Do not paint *things*, paint the conditions in which things are, the light and the reflections in the atmosphere. The thing is temporary and decays, but the conditions have always been and will remain true." In her living room hangs a Bohm painting of a becalmed dory tethered on a slack line in the lower portion of the canvas, while the whole upper portion is vast with blue atmosphere weighing like a shadow upon an image of emptiness.

Packard's sense of scale is similar, and her paintings are particularly effective when the frame she chooses seems too small for all she has to say.

Quick Tuna Casserole

1 can tuna
1 can mushroom soup
1 box Uncle Ben's Wild Rice
 Mixture, cooked
3 heaping tablespoons
 chopped green pepper
1 medium onion, chopped
⅓ cup milk
4 stuffed eggs
a shake of red pepper sauce
potato chips

Throw the tuna, soup, cooked rice, chopped pepper, chopped onion, and milk in a casserole and mix together. Season with salt and a shake of red pepper sauce. Then gently bury the 8 halves of egg in the mixture. Cover the top with potato chips. Bake at 350° until heated through, 20 to 30 minutes.

Red Kidney Bean Salad

1 1-lb. can red kidney beans, drained and rinsed
1 white onion, finely chopped
1 garlic clove, minced
1 to 3 tablespoons olive oil
1 tablespoon wine vinegar
¼ teaspoon mustard
salt to taste
2 pinches of curry powder

Empty the beans into a deep dish. Mix in the onion and garlic. Combine the remaining ingredients to make a vinaigrette and pour it on the beans. Stir, cover, and let the salad stand overnight—but not in the refrigerator, where it is too cold for the flavor to develop.

Pine Nut Pie

Much better than pecan pie—and lighter.

3 eggs, beaten slightly
1 cup light Karo syrup
¾ cup sugar
3 tablespoons butter, melted
1 teaspoon vanilla extract
1 cup pine nuts
1 uncooked pie shell

Mix thoroughly the eggs, syrup, sugar, butter and vanilla extract. Then add the nuts and pour the mixture into the pie shell. Bake at 350° for 45 to 50 minutes. Cool at room temperature and serve with whipped cream or ice cream.

Jay Critchley succeeds as a performance artist, not because he performs so well, since there are many moments when he falters, arousing our anxiety, but because he arouses our anxiety over whether what he does is art. He performs in various media. He dances, speaks, sings, founds organizations, presides over ceremonies, creates ceremonies involving social issues such as acid rain and AIDS, writes proposals, conducts a series of radio interviews with artists, writes press releases, draws in sand wearing the costume of Indian sand painters, acts, makes collages with fish skins, and has covered a fully registered station wagon with sand. This car-as-sculpture was left legally parked during the summer of 1981 in the town parking lot adjacent to MacMillan Wharf, where many of tourists passed by, Critchley thus claiming a huge attendance at the municipal space which he had transformed into a "gallery."

Several years ago Critchley aroused notable controversy when he exhibited a mock Statue of Liberty—the arm reaching to the ceiling of the Art Association, a gas mask over the face—wearing a crown and gown fashioned from 3,000 plastic tampon applicators, refuse that had been collected from the beaches. Critchley's "Lady of Shame" stood still on a pedestal amid the incessant, tape-recorded sound of a toilet flushing. A mirrored-ball light circled the room, making the statue look like a pathetic housewife on "Queen for a Day," grinning for joy at the announcement that she has won a new mop. An artist exhibiting on a wall adjacent to Critchley complained that his work was subjected to the revolving light, which floated across his colors like so many handfuls of confetti. Nodding sympathy to the offended artist, while clucking that the aesthetics of bad taste were unappreciated, Critchley accused his feminist critics of "dishonoring" tampon applicators by deeming them unworthy of being used in a work of art, begging the question of what a work of art is.

Doubtless the scholastic paradoxes inherent in Critchley's work, involving the audience reaction as part of the piece, stem from his early training as an altar boy. His family had been chosen "Catholic Family of the Year" in Connecticut. He went to Mass every day. On Holy Days, he would be in Church for 12 hours, serving at the altar. "My ideal," he confesses, "was to be a priest." After graduating from a Jesuit college, he worked as a counsellor, where he learned that "people in the helping professions often are seeking help themselves. That's what happened to me!" He arrived in Provincetown 18 years ago, married. Soon he became a father, came out of the closet as a homosexual, divorced, quit smoking and drinking, began eating vegetables, and started producing art. Sand appears throughout his work, as a spiritual symbol, "because sand is everywhere," he says.

Critchley's love of ritual extends into the kitchen, where the bread is covered with sand. He admires it as fine sculpture. In the recipe that follows, he offers us not consumption for the stomach, but food for thought. Enjoy!

Third World Pate

"If we expect them to become civilized, we must offer them more enticing and nutritious dishes of proven value like **Third World Pate,** *" writes energetic First Lady Nancy Reagan in her popular Just Say No Diet Cookbook. This dish is always a knockout at socially-conscious gatherings. It provides an opportunity for busy yet concerned professionals to "Just Say No" to expensive and trendy foods, while popularizing the proven worth of pate in Third World countries. And isn't it time they ate as well as our pets!*

2 6-oz. cans of cat food, liver preferred, but seafood or salmon provides an unusual variation or 4 3-oz. cans of Family Feast Gourmet Cat Food, if desired
salt, pepper, paprika to taste
splash of cognac, though use of an indigenous liquor is encouraged
6 pita breads

Remove the cat food from the cans. Add the seasonings and cognac. Mix thoroughly. Cut the pita breads into 2-inch pieces. Serve the pate in a small bowl, surrounded by pita slices, in a candlelit, primitive setting.

Carol Whorf Westcott says she can see something of her brushwork and color in her paintings that reminds her of her father's fluid watercolors, yet she insists, "I have a long way to go to have his clear vision." Her father, John Whorf, according to a catalogue published by the Provincetown Art Association, was Provincetown's most successful artist immediately after World War II and just prior to the heyday of the arriving Abstract Expressionists. Selling out his first one-man show at the age of 21, including a painting to John Singer Sargent, Whorf later worked exclusively in watercolor, painting barges tethered gloomily to a breathing fog or attractive women bathing nude in some secret spot in nature, all rendered with joy and exuberance. Recognized by his ever-present yachting cap, movie-star handsome, Whorf embodied the romance of the artist enjoying his life. During the days when the Art Association had exhibitions that segregated "modern" artists from "traditional" artists, Whorf played a practical joke by painting an abstract picture blindfolded (he was assisted by Richard Miller), signing it "Ad Wolgast," and submitting it successfully to the jury, Wolgast winning praise in a newspaper review for his "great promise." "My father knew how to paint a picture," Carol Westcott counters. "Why shouldn't he be able to paint an abstract one?"

When she was 18, Westcott left Provincetown and attended the Rhode Island School of Design for one year. She married a Marine Corps officer, Charlie Westcott, also from Provincetown, and spent the next 15 years on military bases in various parts of the country. Raising six children, she cooked for all, "because family comes first." As a painter, she got started again, at age 35 while living in El Paso, Texas, "painting little heads of children," then, in Washington, she took classes at the Corcoran, where she was struck by the importance of drawing and structure. Returning to Provincetown in 1977, after her husband's retirement, Westcott says, "It's not easy going back to a town you grew up in. It took me several years to quit complaining about the overdevelopment." She has since become a prolific artist who cherishes the smallness of her studio, tucked away in the shadow of a tall condominium, saying, "My father never needed more than a room to paint." Her focus as an artist is on a reasoned compromise between color and structure. She relies particularly on a deft play of shadows on scenery, giving the painting a secondary composition that echoes abstractly what is presented realistically. Recently she has become intrigued by the artist-model relationship and has been painting portraits of Provincetown friends, such as Anthony Jackett, a veteran fisherman and former owner of *The Plymouth Belle*. Her portrait, reproduced here, shows Jackett detached from his past, his eyes looking into the beyond as if remembering the fisherman's prayer that begins, "O Lord, the ocean is so large and my boat is so small."

Barley

Most of my favorite recipes came from friends during our time in the Marine Corps — so I would say that it's a fair sampling of recipes from all over the United States.

1 cube butter or margarine
1¾ cups pearl barley
2 medium onions, chopped
1 lb. mushrooms, sliced
1 cup water
  (if canned mushrooms are
  used, add liquid to make
  one cup)
4 cups chicken stock or
  6 bouillon cubes dissolved
  in 4 cups water
slivered almonds

Melt half of the butter in a metal frying pan. Pour in the barley and cook until golden brown. Pour into a large casserole dish. Add two more tablespoons of butter and saute the onions until they are clear. Add them to the barley and stir in. Use the rest of the butter to saute the mushrooms and add them to the barley. Combine the mushroom liquid and stock, and pour two cups of the liquid over the barley. Cover the casserole tightly and bake for 45 minutes at 350°. Add two more cups of liquid, stir, and bake for another 45 minutes. Add the remaining liquid and the slivered almonds and cook for 30 minutes longer.

Flank Steak

Flank steak tends to be cheaper than most other cuts of steak and will go farther.

1 flank steak
½ jar Roka cheese
1 clove garlic, mashed
½ cup Italian dressing

Pierce the flank steak with a fork about every inch. Marinate the steak in Italian dressing for two hours. Pat dry. Mix the cheese and mashed garlic together and spread on one side of the flank steak. Roll up the meat with the garlic mixture on the inside, starting with the long side, and tie it with string at one inch intervals. Return the rolled steak to the marinade to coat both sides. Barbecue the flank steak over coals, or oven broil, brushing with marinade periodically. Serves 2 or 3.

"Provincetown Garden," oil on canvas

Pineapple Mint Supreme

This was a Pillsbury Bake-off winner about 25 years ago.

1 cup flour
½ cup chopped walnuts
¼ cup firmly packed brown
sugar
½ cup butter
1 large can crushed
pineapple (1 lb. 4 oz.)
1 package lime gelatin
8 oz. package cream cheese
1 cup sugar
⅔ cup evaporated milk
1/8 teaspoon peppermint

Glaze:
½ cup chocolate bits
⅓ cup evaporated milk
1 tablespoon peppermint

Combine the flour, chopped walnuts and brown sugar. Cut in the butter finely. Press mixture into the bottom of a greased dish 12 x 8 x 2 and bake at 400° for 12 to 15 minutes. Let cool.

Filling: Drain the pineapple juice into a pan and bring juice to a boil. Dissolve the gelatin into the juice and let it cool. Cream together the cream cheese and sugar and blend in the gelatin; stir in the pineapple pieces and chill until mixture is thick.

Chill the evaporated milk and peppermint until crystals form. Then beat until thick and fold into the pineapple mixture. Pour into the cooled crust.

For the glaze, melt ½ cup chocolate bits with the evaporated milk and one tablespoon peppermint. Make sure you add enough milk so that the glaze will dribble easily over the dessert. Chill at least four hours before serving. Serves 12.

When Bruce McKain was attending the John Herron Art School in Indianapolis, in a portrait class he found he was having trouble painting hands. He painted hands that were waxy and dead. He had seen the hands of Provincetown fishermen, painted by Charles Hawthorne, in the Indianapolis Art Museum. A fellow art school student, Sandy Selfridge, had spent two summers in Provincetown studying with Hawthorne, and he told McKain about the charismatic founder of the Cape Cod School of Art. By bringing out the rawness in the hard life of the fishermen, Hawthorne gave dignity to their deformities, giving a rosy glow to skin cancer and animating the thick-fingered, tool-like hands of lifelong fishermen, so that they looked damaged by hard use, numbed by cold, yet swollen with power and sympathy. "Wondering how Hawthorne painted the hands he did," McKain recalls, "I saw a notice on the art school bulletin board advertising his school in July and August." He borrowed one hundred dollars on his life insurance and hitchhiked to Provincetown.

By 1932 he was living yearround in Provincetown in a drafty studio at Days Lumberyard. He kept the stove burning with coal "liberated" from the railroad yard, never thinking of stealing from his generous landlord, Frank Days, whose stockpile of coal lay closer at hand in the bins now used as studios by the Fine Arts Work Center. In that time, all the leading artists of Provincetown were members of the Beachcombers, including Edwin Dickinson, Richard Miller and John Whorf. "You met all your friends on Saturday night, put on little plays and sang sea chanteys about somebody's mother who ran a boarding house. Good dinners were 35 cents. It was Prohibition and prune juice, what they called 'shine, was made out of prune juice and run through a still. Fighting liquor. One winter was particularly gamey, as Ed Dickinson said.

It was the practice to invite the officers of the Navy on shore leave. I remember very well the night the cook got interested in the drinking and at nine o'clock the cabbage for the corned beef hadn't yet gone in. Somebody had brought straight alcohol, which went like water. There were different whiskies. George Yater came in with his eyes slightly crossed and watered his whiskey with straight alcohol. Still, we ate dinner that night; then we won the war."

Beef Stew

1 medium onion,
  chopped fine
1 medium green pepper,
  chopped fine,
6 or 8 large mushrooms,
  sliced
1 tablespoon butter
1 tablespoon olive oil
3 lbs. chuck, cut into
  small pieces
3 carrots, chopped
3 celery stalks, chopped
1 16-oz. can stewed tomatoes
1 cup Burgundy
1 bay leaf
salt and pepper to taste

In a large casserole, simmer the onion, green pepper, and mushrooms in the butter and olive oil. Add the beef and saute briefly. Cover and cook gently for 15 minutes. Add the carrots, celery, stewed tomatoes, and Burgundy to the casserole. Stir well. Season to taste and add the bay leaf. Cover the casserole and cook in the oven at 350° until the meat is tender, about 1½ hours. Serves 6.

Baked Pork Chops

4 pork chops
4 heaping tablespoons
  Pepperidge Farm stuffing
milk
2 apples
raisins

Place the chops in a baking pan. Mix the stuffing with a little milk. Cover each chop with the stuffing. Cut the apples in half. Remove the cores and fill the resulting holes with raisins. Place half an apple on each chop, flat side down. Bake at 400° for one hour. Reduce the heat to 350° for another half an hour. Potatoes can be baked along with the chops. Serves 4.

Hot Rum

For each drink:
half a lemon
1 teaspoon brown sugar
hot water
rum

Squeeze the lemon for its juice. Add a spoonful of brown sugar to the lemon juice. Add a little hot water and rum according to tolerance.

Betty Bodian came to Provincetown in romantic anticipation after she had seen Bette Davis fall in love in a Hollywood movie about Cape Cod, the story set between the slanting evening shadows that fall on the sunny cliffs of Cape Cod's outer beaches, with the fog rolling in and the dark color seeping through the sand like ink into thirsty paper. As an artist, Bodian saw a sensuality in the act of painting, which was like an erotic thrill felt by trespassing lovers, coloring the place with the stain of their presence. In the fifties, when she made actual acquaintance with Provincetown, she recalls the "beautiful, breezy" bonfires and parties that took place near Boris Margo's shack on the back shore, bonfires now forbidden by the National Seashore. Each August, Margo would organize a Midsummer's Night celebration. "He would get a fire permit and we would have a bonfire four or five stories high. An enormous pile of driftwood had to be gathered for this pyre, which took a tremendous amount of cooperation, really a type of social activity spilling over from art openings and Happenings that were taking place all over town. Around the big bonfire we all made smaller fires."

Bodian is a founding member of the Group Gallery, Provincetown's oldest artist's co-op. Her early work showed images of the seashore, seen from a distance through throbs of heat waves, lazy, reclining figures in bikinis and less, their shapes essentialized in sure colors that fall softly as cloth on cloth. Her collages of thickly saturated torn papers are undisguised in their gratitude to Matisse, for showing a way for art to be frankly, openly hedonistic. While she has summered in Provincetown for over 30 years, she has lived in New York on Second Avenue near St. Mark's Place, long before the area became known as the East Village. Her paintings of the street life there were exhibited recently at the Group Gallery after a long hiatus making purely abstract collages. They witness the evolution of the East Village from a bum's row to a carnival where entrance columns of decaying buildings are painted pink and pale green. The punks parade in leather, feathers, and masks, like actors in a street threater that co-exists with any live art scene.

Betty Bodian's Seviche

2 lbs. flounder or any
  whitefish fillet (*not* cod), cut
  in large bite-size pieces
2 limes, juiced
1 medium or large red onion,
  chopped
2 ripe tomatoes, chopped, or
  1 can baby sliced tomatoes
1 cup green pepper,
  chopped
chopped parsley, about
  a handful
¼ cup olive oil
¼ cup red wine vinegar
½ teaspoon oregano
1 jalapeno pepper,
  chopped fine
  or ½ jar Progresso
  pepper salad, cut up, with
  some oil from the jar

Macerate the fish in the lime juice for six hours, or overnight. Toss a few times to make sure all the fish is coated in lime juice. When all fish has turned white, remove half the liquid. Add the onion, tomatoes, green pepper, and parsley to the fish.

In a small bowl, combine the olive oil, vinegar, oregano, jalapeno pepper *or* pepper salad, and add to the marinated fish mixture. Refrigerate for 3 or 4 hours; stir two or three times before serving and serve well chilled.

The texture changes as it pickles. It is best eaten when it is fresh, but "done." This amount will serve eight generously as a first course, or 12 as cocktail-party nibble. In my experience, people eat every last morsel of this salad, so accompany it with plenty of chunks of baguette, tortillas, or corn chips.

Bayberry Swordfish Marinade

This recipe is a variation of a Greek style of grilled swordfish. Originally, this marinade was created for a shish kebab of 1½" cubes of swordfish, when, in the early '60s, we were able to buy the stuff for 69¢ a pound. It can just as easily flavor ¾" steaks, but the marinating time should be shortened. The bayberry called for here has a taste similar to, but weaker than, the bay leaf.

2 cups bayberry leaves, from
  a clean, unpolluted place
  (Provincetown)
  without berries
1 large white onion,
  coarsely chopped
4 garlic cloves, chopped
1 handful of parsley, chopped
salt & ground black pepper
½ cup olive oil
½ cup red wine vinegar
swordfish, cut in cubes
skewers for grilling

Wash the bayberry leaves and combine with the onion, garlic, parsley, salt and pepper, olive oil, and vinegar. Marinate the swordfish in this mixture. (Remember not to over marinate the thinner version. I used to give the big cubes no more than six hours.) Thread the cubes on skewers with bits of bayberry leaves and onion clinging to them, and grill over an even charcoal fire. The steaks may also be grilled on a grate covered by perforated foil.

The granddaughter of Henry Varnum Poor, an artist who spent long summers in Truro memorably painting the Pamet Valley, Anna Poor has the sensibility of a landscape artist in her blood. Her own work incorporates vistas less seen than dreamed. She works in wood, carving and chopping stubbornly until she has fashioned her images into something more permanent than the impressions we receive during REM sleep. Implicitly accepting Freud's discovery that the unconscious cannot express the negative except through positive images, she is utterly modern in her presentation of conflict. "No," "never," "absence" and "fear," are concepts she expresses symbolically in the ambivalent manner of dreams, where the meaning is bundled in a knot of associations. (A woman in love with a sailor who is away at sea might dream of knots and her sailor who is *not* there.) Perhaps the supreme form for 20th century expression of discontinuities is collage, and it is plausible to think of Anna Poor's bas reliefs and totems as a type of carved collage, where fleeting, evanescent and momentary feelings are placed spatially side by side with something of the solidarity of Greek friezes and columns.

For the work reproduced in this book, titled "Hieroglyphics," she has kindly offered an explication. Insisting that her pieces are "*not* 'domestic' or 'whimsical,'" she says that the globe is the chance location of birth; that

butter, martinis, olives and cigarettes are food in its decadent or lustful aspect, while the coffee cup and saltines are a modern equivalent of bread and water, or food in its aspect of providing survival; that the lifesaver is a small sign of hope, the islands are the unknown, and the knife is a weapon either of destruction or self-defense. Be that as it may, the interpretation of her images, as in the interpretation of dreams, depends less on a process of inert decoding than on a response to the implications of her expressions, for example, how the globe floats small like an alien planet within the familiar landscape of the planet Earth, at once suspended in the sky, buoyant upon the water and balanced upon a cloud of smoke from the cigarette burning beneath it.

"Hieroglyphics," painted wood construction

Sweet Potato Pie

3 sweet potatoes
½ cup light brown sugar
¼ cup dark brown sugar
½ teaspoon each cinnamon, mace, salt, and ginger
3 eggs
1½ cups light cream
an unbaked pie crust
sweetened whipped cream

All measurements are approximate.

Preheat oven to 400°. Cook and mash the sweet potatoes; set aside. Mix together in a bowl the light and dark brown sugars; add the cinnamon, mace, salt, and ginger. Beat in the eggs. Stir in the potatoes (about 1 cup) and the light cream. Pour the mixture into an uncooked pie crust and bake for about 50 minutes or until you can stick a knife in and it comes out clean. Cool. Top with sweetened whipped cream.

Scallops with Vegetables

1 lb. scallops
½ cup milk
flour
2 tablespoons butter
½ lb. mushrooms, sliced
½ cup scallions, chopped
¼ cup parsley, chopped
red pepper flakes to taste
a sprinkling of black pepper
a wine glass of white wine
fresh lemon juice

Soak the scallops in milk and drain (give the milk to the cats). Lightly and quickly dust the scallops in flour. Do this seconds before you put them in a heavy frying pan that has hot, browned butter in it. (If they sit around with the flour on them, they may become gummy.)

After the scallops are nicely browned (do not overcook), remove them from the pan. Add more butter to the pan and saute the mushrooms, scallions, parsley, and a little red pepper. (You may add other things if you wish, like peas and tofu, depending on what's on hand.) Add black pepper. Return the scallops to the pan of vegetables, pour in some white wine, simmer for about 5 minutes, squeeze on some lemon, and serve with a lot of rice.

Vico Fabbris was born in northern Italy in 1950 and studied both art and "publicity graphics" in Florence. By the time he had received a degree in painting from L'Accademia di Belle Arti, he had already been commissioned to do four murals. The largest, for the University of Florence, measures 15 feet by 140 feet. Another, his "most rewarding," was done while working with patients in the Psychiatric Hospital of San Salvi. Since 1980, he has been spending long summers in Provincetown. He tends a quiet garden under shady trees high up Atkens-Mayo Road, cultivating herbs, drying them, and grinding together mixtures of four or five herbs. On occasion he will prepare special dishes for his friend and neighbor, Sal Del Deo, which will be served at Sal's restaurant, the hostess explaining that they contain "secret herbs." His paintings have been exhibited at the Cherry Stone Gallery, the Group Gallery, the Art Association, and currently at the David Brown Gallery. For a number of years he has shared households with Grace Consoli, a photographer and gallery director, who has been recording the costumes and masks during Carnevale in Venice as well as conducting a Florence radio program, "Artemisia," with interviews with Georg Baselitz and Enzo Cucchi, among others.

Like many artists involved in "appropriating" previous styles, Vico is aware that the present glory of Florence is in its past. His work is contemporary with a classical theme, such as "Struggle of the Artist,"

Grace Consoli

reproduced in this book, portraying the artist in his quest to overcome the process of creativity. "It is fine if one acquires success and money," Vico says, "but it should never be looked for, so as not to influence the work that is, and should be, free of its temptation."

Pate di Olive

When Necee Regis visited us in Florence, we made this as an appetizer and she loved it. It is now being served to her guests in Boston. It's very simple to make and is wonderful spread on crackers or bread.

8 oz. green olives, marinated
olive oil
a couple of garlic cloves
chopped parsley
red pepper flakes

Remove the pits from the olives and place the olive meat in a blender with enough extra virgin olive oil to bind the pate, garlic (to taste), fresh parsley, red hot pepper flakes, and other fresh herbs of choice. Blend together to a paste.

There are many variations, depending on one's taste and imagination: black olives can be used; or chopped spinach, tomatoes, and mushrooms instead of olives.

Pasta alla Cardinale

1 lb. pasta — macaroni,
ravioli or tortellini
1 28-oz. or 32-oz. can
peeled tomatoes
3 garlic cloves,
approximately, crushed
4 tbsp. extra virgin olive oil
fresh basil leaves
1 carton cream or
half-and-half
salt and pepper
½ cup grated Parmesan
cheese

Remove any excess peel or hard core from the canned tomatoes, crush them, and pour them into a pot. Add the garlic and two or three basil leaves, and cook until the tomato mixture becomes condensed. When the tomato sauce is done, stir in the olive oil. Leave to simmer while you prepare the pasta.
Fill a spaghetti pot ¾ full of salted water. Bring to a boil and add the pasta of your choice. Cook until *al dente*. Drain the pasta and return it to the pot. Add the tomato sauce, stir, and gradually add the cream while stirring, until the sauce becomes a rose color. Add the grated cheese, freshly ground pepper, stir briskly, and serve immediately. Serves 4.

Risotto alla Milanese

The legend goes that a painter was working on the frescos in the Duomo di Milano and, while he was eating a rice dish for lunch, some yellow pigment accidentally fell into his dish! Angry, but hungry, he stirred quickly and created one of the most famous risotto dishes. Great art is sometimes an accident.

1 lb. Arborio rice
1 medium white onion, chopped
1 quart vegetable or chicken broth
½ glass dry white wine
4 oz. grated Parmesan cheese (about)
butter, about 2 oz.
extra virgin olive oil
1 tiny envelope saffron (about 2 grams)

In a medium-sized pot, saute the onion in the olive oil until transparent. Add the rice and stir for a couple of minutes. Add the broth gradually to the rice until it is just covered, and stir. As the rice cooks and the broth gets absorbed, keep adding broth, just to keep the rice covered with liquid until it is cooked. Add the wine when the rice is ¾ cooked, and stir. When the rice is done, add butter to taste, the grated cheese, and the saffron, which has been dissolved in a little hot water or broth. Stir energetically and let the risotto rest for about five minutes before serving. The rice should not be too dry or too soupy. The whole process should take about 25 minutes. Serves 4.

Pollo alla Birra

1 chicken, cut into small pieces
1 medium white onion, chopped
2 or 3 garlic cloves, chopped
1 or 2 bottles of light beer
1½ chicken bouillon cubes
extra virgin olive oil
fresh sage and rosemary
salt and pepper

In a pot that is deep and wide enough to hold the chicken in a single layer, saute the onion and garlic in some olive oil until they become translucent. Add the chicken pieces and cook until they become white, about five minutes; turn them. Then pour in the beer until the chicken is covered and boil for a few minutes. Add the bouillon cubes in small pieces so they dissolve. Add the sage, rosemary, salt and pepper to taste.

On a low flame, let the chicken simmer, half covered, for about 20 minutes, occasionally turning it. If the chicken isn't cooked by the time the beer is fully absorbed, gradually add more beer. The chicken should not stick to the pan and should be accompanied by its own sauce.

Zabaglione

Creativity and fantasy is important in cooking. Add more or less, but do it from the heart and it will be good.

per person:

1 egg yolk
sugar
Marsala

In a small pot, combine the egg yolk, sugar to taste (approximately three tablespoons), and two half egg shells of Marsala. Beat with a whisk on a very low flame until the mixture becomes fluffy. Serve as a topping for fresh berries or spoon into wine goblets and sprinkle grated chocolate on top. Zabaglione may be served warm or chilled.

Variation: use white wine instead of Marsala, grate nutmeg, then mix together.

"Struggle of the Artist," acrylic on paper

Jane Kogan is one of the many
Fellows of the Fine Arts Work Center
who, after introduction to Provincetown through the period of their
fellowship, chose to stay on and live
in the community. In her employment
at the Provincetown Bookshop,
Kogan keeps the small store window
densely packed with new publica-
tions, such as poetry by a poet that
week giving a reading at Napi's, or a
Cape Light calendar for the forthcoming year by Joel Meyerowitz, or
a children's book by Howie Schneider
and Susan Seligson about their dog
and its travels on a magical couch.

Kogan attended New York City's
High School of Music and Art. She
graduated *magna cum laude* from
Brandeis, attended the Art Student's
League on scholarship, spent two
years in Rome on a Fulbright and
received an MFA from Columbia. "As
a child of the city," she says, "my
obsession has always been with
people, their psychology." Recently,
at the Ellen Harris Gallery in Provincetown, Kogan showed a series of portraits
of friends, sitting composed and courageous against a vigilant wash of light
that was like an interrogation of the person's skin, baring his soul. She says,
"For me, art is creative play whose serious purpose is a shaped response to
the world as we find it. Part of the challenge of portraits is the intimacy
between artist and model, an emotional and intellectual interplay that is like a
game. The artist tries to get behind the surface of the sitter's mind, to put that
too on canvas. It's a kind of invasive procedure by mutual consent, the sitter
willing to be explored, the artist incisive enough to see."

A nude body can present itself artistically as a metaphor for nakedness,
and Kogan's self-portraits of herself in the nude, wearing nothing but her
eyeglasses, are sexy in the wholesome way that art can be erotic. Kogan
offers, not herself, but her art.

Tomato Bisque

Here's my solution for what to do with all those luscious ripe tomatoes friends give me from their gardens in late September before they leave the Cape.

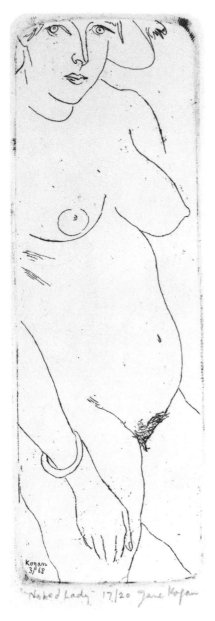

6 large tomatoes,
   cut into chunks
1 medium onion, diced fine
fresh parsley, several sprigs,
   finely chopped
1 bay leaf
pepper to taste
Tabasco
1 teaspoon mustard seed
tarragon
⅔ tablespoon brown sugar
⅓ teaspoon curry powder
1 cup milk or cream
⅛ teaspoon baking soda

Place chopped tomatoes and onion in a heavy pot with enough water to cover the bottom. Cook, covered, until you can mash the vegetables (about 10–15 minutes). Meanwhile, chop the parsley fine. Add it (or a scant tablespoon parsley flakes may be substituted), the bay leaf, pepper, a few drops of Tabasco, mustard seed, pinch of tarragon, brown sugar, and curry powder to the tomato mixture. Cook uncovered on low heat until all the flavors are well blended. Then add the milk or cream, stirring constantly. (A pinch of baking soda added to tomato mixture will prevent the milk from curdling when it is added.) Serves 2 to 3 amply.

"Naked Lady," etching

Hamburger with Cabbage

When I was back in New York City, living hand to mouth on almost nothing back in the 1960s, this was a recipe I often made and enjoyed. It astonishes me, now, to see how much our eating patterns have changed in the past 25 years. And hamburger, that used to be 29¢–39¢ per pound! So this was a really cheap dish.

1 ripe tomato
1 small onion
⅓ sweet red pepper
1 carrot (optional)
⅓ lb. hamburger (or chicken livers)
½ small cabbage, chopped
Worcestershire sauce
chili powder
sour cream

Cut the tomato into chunks, dice the onion, slice the red pepper into strips, cut the carrot in bite-sized rounds. Put the vegetables in a heavy frying pan, add the hamburger, and cover, cooking over low-medium flame to steam. Stir occasionally to break up any lumps. (The vegetables should provide enough liquid for steaming.)

Meanwhile, steam the cabbage. Add Worcestershire sauce and chili powder to taste to the meat–vegetable mixture. When the cabbage is cooked, combine it in a soup plate with the hamburger mixture and mix in the sour cream, stirring through; or add a dollop on top, whichever you prefer. Serves one.

Almond Slab Biscuits

And finally, here's a no-fail simple recipe given me by my father's wife, Wini. I've doctored it only a little.

½ lb. butter, softened
2 cups flour
½ cup sugar
1 egg
slivered almonds (approximately 2 oz.)
a few drops almond or vanilla flavoring (optional)

Cream together the butter, flour, and sugar. Add the flavoring, if used. Spread the mixture thinly and evenly on a 10'' × 15'' cookie sheet. Beat the egg, and thoroughly brush it over the entire top of the dough.

Sprinkle or lay out the slivered almonds evenly, pressing each lightly into the dough. Bake at 300° for 20–30 minutes, until the top is golden.

Cut into squares (I usually get about 30) while still warm. Put in the refrigerator to cool before eating; otherwise they crumble.

FRANK MILBY

Frank Milby paints pictures of familiar waterfront scenes — fishing boats, seagulls and other motifs that are locally elected to prominent attention by the majority of the community, in the same way that the old wall hung with painted buoys, called "Motif #1," is the visual focus of the art colony at Rockport, Massachusetts. The Provincetown landmark that has most caught the attention of realistic artists is the massive gray building at the end of MacMillan Pier, a fishpacking plant just recently torn down, to the disappointment of many local artists. The building was two stories high, more than a hundred feet long, and was composed of many numbers of cement blocks. It loomed heavily, swayed in storms, tottering upon the knobby stilts of the wharf's pilings. A favorite subject of such artists as Bruce McKain, Paul Resika and Arthur Cohen, it was also a favorite of Milby's, who loves to paint with grays and browns, making the two dull colors each deepen the resonance of the other. Often seen through fog from a far distance to the east, the building was usually painted by Milby as if it were a dense mark with little detailing, in scale looming as a single tone of potential motion, like the streak of a locomotive painted darkly. In order to relieve stress on the wharf, the building was torn down in the fall of 1987. "Now they have taken the fishhouse," Milby says, "Goodbye to Motif #2."

Frank Milby at the Beachcombers

Jim Zimmerman

Born in Queens, Milby did his time doing street portraits in Greenwich Village and New Orleans. He moved to Provincetown 20 years ago, initially working as a portrait artist at the "Starving Artist Studio." He has since won his reputation as a popular painter of local scenes, and is represented by Trees Gallery in Orleans and by Phoenix Gallery in Provincetown. There is also a less Milbyesque side to Frank Milby—an ongoing series of portraits of black people, usually depicting an isolated brown figure floating in a field of gray. "You want to paint ten things," he says, "but to paint you have to consolidate, so I am always painting the same painting. I like to paint black people, I don't know why." Milby will sometimes paint a brown tree looking lonely and forlorn in a gray empty atmosphere, so that you feel his sympathy for the tree's isolation. Even tempered, ever serene, he observes, "there is great solace in trees. If you're upset, go sit under a tree for half an hour."

Frank Milby, a quintessential member of the Beachcombers, commands a great view of Provincetown harbor from his top floor studio at the Hulk, as the Beachcombers' building is called by members. When a new member joins the Beachcombers, he is accepted only by a unanimous vote of *nays*, typifying the belief that only the symbolic outcast can be a true Beachcomber. "I'll probably leave Provincetown when the Beachcombers get squeezed out," Milby says. A history of the Beachcombers written by Ted Robinson carries the epigraph: "For the Beachcomber, when not a mere ruffian, is the poor relation of the Artist." Milby is rather an artist who disguises himself as the artist's poor relation, dressing even for his daily tennis game in torn, paint-spattered t-shirts (sometimes turned inside out if they have not been too recently washed), wearing instead of tennis shorts whatever pants he has been wearing earlier in the studio, and sometimes (though not always) wearing tennis shoes. Playing at the Provincetown Tennis Club, where the rules are responsive to the idiosyncrasies of its regulars (rule nine reads: "Women are not encouraged to play without shirts"), Milby breaks no dress code.

Mushroom Pie with Oysters or Clams

The Pie Crust:
1 stick butter
1½ cups flour
cold water

The Filling:
1 lb. mushrooms, sliced
grated cheese (Cheddar or mozzarella)
oysters or clams, shucked
chopped parsley and oregano, to taste

To make the crust: crumble the butter into the flour. Add enough cold water to make a smooth dough, then roll it out. Put it in a greased pie plate. Place several pats of butter on the bottom of the crust.

To make the filling: combine ingredients in proportions of your choice. Fill the shell with the mushroom-shellfish mixture, top with the herbs, and bake the pie for 45 minutes at 350°, until the crust is brown and the juices are oozing.

Serve with chilled white wine.

Baby Lima Bean Soup

2 cups lima beans, dried
2 or 3 carrots, sliced
2 potatoes, diced
1 onion, chopped
garlic cloves, minced
½ stick butter
½ pint light cream

Soak the lima beans; wash and drain them. Cover the beans with water and cook until they are tender, approximately one hour. Add the carrots and potatoes, and simmer until tender, for about 20 minutes. In a separate pan, saute the chopped onions and garlic in butter. Add to the soup, stir in the cream, and heat through gently before serving.

"Waterfront," oil

Vegetable Casserole

6 potatoes, grated
2 or 3 carrots, grated
1 large yellow onion, grated
2 or 3 garlic cloves, sliced
2 or 3 eggs, beaten
¼ cup olive oil
salt and pepper
a handful of bread crumbs
a handful of mushrooms,
    chopped
Cheddar or mozzarella
    cheese, grated

Press the grated potatoes, carrots, and onions with the palm of your hand (or use a plate) to squeeze out the juices. Pour off the liquid. Layer the vegetables in a big, flat pan, add the eggs, oil, garlic, salt and pepper, and sprinkle bread crumbs on top. Sprinkle on the chopped mushrooms and top with the grated cheese. Bake at 350° for one hour, until golden brown. This is good served with yogurt.

Beachcombers' Rum Cake

2 boxes Duncan Hines
  yellow cake mix
2 boxes vanilla pudding mix
1 stick margarine or butter,
  softened
8 eggs, beaten
1 can unsweetened
  sliced pineapple
½ cup rum

Sauce:
2 cups sugar
2 sticks butter
2 cups water
1½ cups rum

2 cartons heavy cream,
  whipped

Use any shape pan large enough to hold the batter; grease and flour the bottom of it. Put the pineapple slices all around the bottom of the pan. Make the batter by combining the first four ingredients and the rum and pineapple juice; pour the batter into the pan. Bake the cake for one hour at 350°. Cool the cake, allowing it to separate from the sides of the pan.

Meanwhile, in a heavy sauce pan, boil the two cups of sugar, the two sticks of butter, and two cups of water; let this mixture thicken, taking care not to let it burn. Add 1½ cups rum and remove from heat.

When the cake is cool and the sauce thick, flip the cake over on a board so the pineapple slices are on top. Slice the cake in half horizontally. Fill the center with whipped cream. Replace the top half of the cake and pour the sauce slowly over it, letting the cake absorb the sauce. Feeds twenty men.

For normal people, not Beachcombers, you could cut this recipe in half; but don't halve the rum.

"Self Portrait," oil